CHANGING MIND-SETS
The Potential Unconscious

PSYCHOANALYTIC CROSSCURRENTS
General Editor: Leo Goldberger

CHANGING MIND-SETS
The Potential Unconscious

Maria Carmen Gear,
Ernesto César Liendo,
and
Lila Lee Scott

NEW YORK UNIVERSITY PRESS
New York and London

Library of Congress Cataloging-in-Publication Data
Gear, Maria Carmen.
Changing mind-sets : the potential unconscious / Maria Carmen
Gear, Ernesto César Liendo, and Lila Lee Scott.
p. cm. — (Psychoanalytic crosscurrents)
Bibliography: p.
Includes index.
ISBN 0-8147-3023-X (alk. paper)
1. Psychotherapy. 2. Psychoanalysis. I. Liendo, Ernesto César.
II. Scott, Lila Lee. III. Title. IV. Series.
RC480.5.G43   1989
616.89'14—dc19   89-30112
                                                                        CIP

New York University Press books are printed on acid-free paper,
and their binding materials are chosen for strength and durability.

Psycho-analysis brings forward so much that is new, and among it so much that contradicts traditional opinions and wounds deeply-rooted feelings, that it is bound at first to provoke denial. A reader who suspends his judgement and allows psycho-analysis as a whole to make its impression on him will perhaps become open to a conviction that even this undesired novelty is worth knowing and is indispensable for anyone who wishes to understand the mind and human life.

Sigmund Freud
Introductory lectures on psycho-analysis

CONTENTS

FOREWORD

The *Psychoanalytic Crosscurrents* series presents selected books and monographs that reveal the growing intellectual ferment within and across the boundaries of psychoanalysis.

Freud's theories and grand-scale speculative leaps have been found wanting, if not disturbing, from the very beginning and have led to a succession of derisive attacks, shifts in emphasis, revisions, modifications, and extensions. Despite the chronic and, at times, fierce debate that has characterized psychoanalysis, not only as a movement but also as a science, Freud's genius and transformational impact on the twentieth century have never been seriously questioned. Recent psychoanalytic thought has been subjected to dramatic reassessments under the sway of contemporary currents in the history of ideas, philosophy of science, epistemology, structuralism, critical theory, semantics, and semiology as well as in sociobiology, ethology, and neurocognitive science. Not only is Freud's place in intellectual history being meticulously scrutinized, his texts, too, are being carefully read, explicated, and debated within a variety of conceptual frameworks and sociopolitical contexts.

The legacy of Freud is perhaps most notably evident within the narrow confines of psychoanalysis itself, the "impossible profession" that has served as the central platform for the promulgation of official orthodoxy. But Freud's contributions—his original radical thrust—reach far beyond the parochial concerns of the clinician psychoanalyst as clinician. His writings touch on a wealth of issues, crossing traditional boundaries—be they situated in the biological, social, or humanistic spheres—that have profoundly altered our conception of the individual and society.

A rich and flowering literature, falling under the rubric of "applied psychoanalysis," came into being, reached its zenith many decades ago, and then almost vanished. Early contributors to this literature, in addition to Freud himself, came from a wide range of backgrounds both within and outside the medical/psychiatric field, many later became psychoanalysts themselves. These early efforts were characteristically reductionistic in their attempt to extrapolate from psychoanalytic theory (often the purely clinical theory) to explanations of phenomena lying at some distance from the clinical. Over the years, academic psychologists, educators, anthropologists, sociologists, political scientists, philosophers, jurists, literary critics, art historians, artists, and writers, among others (with or without formal psychoanalytic training) have joined in the proliferation of this literature.

The intent of the *Psychoanalytic Crosscurrents* series is to apply psychoanalytic ideas to topics that may lie beyond the narrowly clinical, but its essential conception and scope are quite different. The present series eschews the reductionistic tendency to be found in much traditional "applied psychoanalysis." It acknowledges not only the complexity of psychological phenomena but also the way in which they are embedded in social and scientific contexts that are constantly changing. It calls for a dialectical relationship to earlier theoretical views and conceptions rather than a mechanical repetition of Freud's dated thoughts. The series affirms the fact that contributions to and about psychoanalysis have come from many directions. It is designed as a forum for the multidisciplinary studies that intersect with psychoanalytic thought but without the requirement that psychoanalysis necessarily be the starting point or, indeed, the center focus. The criteria for inclusion in the series are that the work be significantly informed by psychoanalytic thought or that it be aimed at furthering our understanding of psychoanalysis in its broadest meaning as theory, practice, and sociocultural phenomenon; that it be of current topical interest and that it provide the critical reader with contemporary insights; and, above all, that it be high-quality scholarship, free of obsolete dogma, banalization, and empty jargon. The author's professional identity and particular theoretical orientation matters only to the extent that such facts may serve to frame the work for the reader, alerting him or her to inevitable biases of the author.

The *Psychoanalytic Crosscurrents* series presents an array of works from the multidisciplinary domain in an attempt to capture the ferment of scholarly activities at the core as well as at the boundaries of psychoanalysis. The books and monographs are from a variety of sources: authors will be psychoanalysts—traditional, neo- and post-Freudian, existential, object relational, Kohutian, Lacanian, etc.—social scientists with quantitative or qualitative orientations to psychoanalytic data, and scholars from the vast diversity of approaches and interests that make up the humanities. The series entertains works on critical comparisons of psychoanalytic theories and concepts as well as philosophical examinations of fundamental assumptions and epistemic claims that furnish the base for psychoanalytic hypotheses. It includes studies of psychoanalysis as literature (discourse and narrative theory) as well as the application of psychoanalytic concepts to literary criticism. It will serve as an outlet for psychoanalytic studies of creativity and the arts. Works in the cognitive and the neurosciences will be included to the extent that they address some fundamental psychoanalytic tenet, such as the role of dreaming and other forms of unconscious mental processes.

It should be obvious that an exhaustive enumeration of the types of works that might fit into the *Psychoanalytic Crosscurrents* series is pointless. The studies comprise a lively and growing literature as a unique domain; books of this sort are frequently difficult to classify or catalog. Suffice it to say that the overriding aim of the editor of this series is to serve as a conduit for the identification of the outstanding yield of that emergent literature and to foster its further unhampered growth.

Leo Goldberger
Professor of Psychology
New York University

ACKNOWLEDGMENTS

We would like to acknowledge the vital contribution made to the writing of this book by our team of collaborators comprised of Felix Reyna, Graciela Borges, Mónica Kornblith, Mary Lander, Gloria Goldszmidt, Betty Abadi, José Enrique Zamora, Jorge Posadas, John Day, and Judy Dunn. We have also benefited from fruitful discussions of the material with our colleagues Clara Kizer, Horacio Etchegoyen, Harry Prosen, Robert Martin, Romano Fiumara, Claudio Neri, Juan Miguel Hoffmann, Carlos Featherston, and Yolanda Márquez.

We further wish to recognize the inspiration given to our work by Thomas Kuhn, Melanie Klein, Wilfred Bion, Jacques Lacan, André Green, Claude Lévi-Strauss, Gregory Bateson, Leon Grinberg, David Liberman, Daniel Glauser, and Mauricio Goldemberg.

INTRODUCTION

This book is about restoring freedom of choice. It addresses the potential of psychoanalysis to increase personal freedom by overcoming the repetition compulsion to which a person may be bound by unconscious motivation. Such an individual repeats old experiences without recognizing them as such, believing that this behavior is motivated by actual circumstances. Treatment focuses on an exploration of historic and social pressures that, along with biological limitations, have conditioned the person's symbolic activity.

In this book, we will show how to make liberation from this compulsion possible. In so doing, we will reconsider certain fundamental hypotheses of Freudian metapsychology in their topical, structural, dynamic, and economic aspects. Using an interdisciplinary perspective enriched by semiotics, problem-solving theory, dual-coding theory, theory of power, and cognitive theory, we will make what we believe is a significant reformulation of Freud's metapsychology and an important shift in the tasks and focus of the therapeutic process.

Freudian theory asks us to attend to material present in the unconscious. We propose that therapy must also attend material that is specifically and notably *absent* from both consciousness and the unconscious. Its absence is evident to the therapist just as a missing piece is obvious to one who must complete a puzzle. What is missing is what is specifically necessary to free desire from the repetition compulsion and to solve the problems that the analysand confronts in his efforts to create happiness. This missing element is not repressed; it is unarticulated to the analysand's system of understanding. Although essential, it is not perceived as significant, commented upon, or evident in the dreams and free associations of the analysand. It could be considered to be repudiated in that it is actively excluded from the structure of the conscious and unconscious systems.

Freud's first topical model (1900) consisted of three psychic spaces: the conscious, unconscious, and preconscious. According to Freud's model, that which the subject does not tolerate remains in the unconscious; that which the superego does not tolerate also remains in the id-unconscious topographic division. In his structural model, the id, with its repressed material, and the superego, with its repressing function, were central points of analysis. The emphasis was placed on making conscious what was already present but was repressed in the unconscious, putting ego where id had been. Repression and conflict were the dynamic problems to be overcome to give the patient a greater freedom to feel, think, and act. It is in this frame of reference that we reformulate metapsychology in all its traditional aspects. We have emphasized the therapeutic material that is not yet articulated to the preconscious, conscious, or unconscious topical spaces. We see this material as represented in a potential space, outside the limits established by the organizing preconscious frame.

The preconscious is pivotal to our model. Other spaces are organized in relation to it. We maintain that the preconscious divides them into two major groupings, *intraframe* and *extraframe*. The conscious and unconscious are *intraframe*, being constricted and organized by the assumptions of the preconscious frame. Beyond these constrictions are two newly defined spaces, the metaconscious and the potential unconscious. The metaconscious is necessary for the perception and examination of the important preconscious organizing assumptions, or the paradigm. The potential unconscious contains representations that are dissonant to these assumptions and are actively excluded from incorporation into the *intraframe* conscious and unconscious spaces. It also contains enriching creative representations that lie beyond the frame constrictions. Both a developed metaconscious space and an enriching potential unconscious space are necessary to the analysand in his efforts to free himself from the limitations of his preconscious frame assumptions. In the structural aspect, the superego is modeled as the "law" and the "legislator," dogmatically defending against changing basic assumptions.

We see the analysand as analogous to a scientist whose freedom to observe is conditioned by his theory, as are the truths that he can prove. The theoretical assumptions are preconscious; they form an informal selective and organizing structure that tends to persist, giving congruence and consistency to isolated individual experience. Since the theory is shared by the significant others in the analysand's environment and tends to be confirmed by them, social resistance is brought to bear on attempts to change a shared paradigm. The emphasis on the preconscious paradigm as an important focus in therapy has resulted in our calling our approach "paradigmatic psychoanalysis."

In the dynamic aspect, we propose as basic the struggle to overcome the symbolic incompetence that results in an overwhelming anxiety called "traumatic anxiety." We have noted that, in defense against this anxiety, our clients reiterated certain themes about blame and devaluation. In our experience, these themes have been obvious in a striking way in the speech and actions of the analysand and consistent regardless of the client's cultural background. Clients seem to use these personal disqualifications to distribute unfairly the displeasure and dissatisfaction they experience because of their own ineffective performances. We have called the defensive use of these personal disqualifications the "melodrama." We observed that patients assumed and assigned to others a stereotyped role. For example, if they felt themselves victims, they assigned to the other the role of victimizer. These scenes were enacted and reenacted compulsively. In such contexts, because patients occupy themselves with guilt and inferiority, they completely ignore problems that affect the quality of their lives and that have to be resolved if they are to find ways to be happy in their love and work. The dramatic problem, although absent from what they relate, is present in the unconscious and is the source of the traumatic anxiety to which the melodrama is a defensive response. Such material may become apparent to the therapist on questioning or as a result of comments of significant others who are aware of the threatened failure.

The melodramatic defense is defined here as compulsively escaping from anxiety while unfairly distributing unhappiness through interpersonal disqualifications. Our analysands escaped immediate anxiety, but incurred the cost of a failure to enrich themselves and to grow beyond their historic limitations. For example, a patient would escape the anxiety of facing an economic failure by constantly blaming his wife for being inferior and incompetent in household tasks. And his wife would simply affirm her guilt, not commenting on the dramatic economic problem that was creating the anxiety and family suffering, and thus help to perpetuate the melodrama.

In many patients, opportunities for finding happiness are passed by, unrecognized, and unvalued. In our experience, when we brought core problems to our patients' attention, they rejected them as "unnatural," using previously learned and established dogmatic criteria to discredit them. In these instances, the therapist's observation had brought to their attention certain material that was foreign to them; it lay beyond the limits of their system of established personal assumptions and of the assumptions that determined the sociopathology expressed in their cultures. It was dissonant material and remained in the *extraframe* potential unconscious, even though it was relevant to the solution of current life problems.

Such a topical and dynamic reconceptualization constitutes the first part of the book. In the second part, we reexamine Freud's model of dual thought processes, primary and secondary, in the light of recent scientific advances that clarify the biological distinction between the right analogic (nondominant) and left digital (dominant) hemispheric coding functions (Nebes 1974). Freud modeled the relationship between the two codes as one of opposition, not of complementarity, and he tended to identify primary process with pathology. We reconsider the healthy and pathological functioning of these dual processes. The right hemispheric analogic process is considered to be primary but is no longer mistakenly identified with the primitive or pathological. Primary takes on the significance of "first" or "before" in that the thing representation which is analogic occurs in coding before the word representation which is digital. Analogic primary process, however, like left hemispheric digital secondary process, is capable of healthy, complex, and elaborate functions, which are also essential in distinct and complementary aspects of problem-solving thinking (Sperry, Gazzaniga, Bogen 1969). A failure to use these modes in a complementary fashion is what is pathological. Excessive development of one coding mode and a deficiency in the complementary mode is related by us to cognitive style. This is itself related to learning style and to certain difficulties that the analysand may consistently experience in his problem-solving efforts.

We have also related recent advances in dual coding models to the affect organizers of constricted conscious and unconscious motivation. In relation to the economic model, Freud conceptualized an affect charge in the deep unconscious that is united to a representation or group of representations. The unification of this charge to its representation was responsible for unconscious motivation. There is now experimental evidence that, just as he intuitively proposed, analogic experiential symbols are directly linked to affect. To break this bonding and reorganize affect meaning is one of the most difficult tasks in liberating unconscious desire.

Freud saw the repetition compulsion as an expression of the death instinct. We see it as a primitive expression of a survival instinct. For us, affect has become strongly bonded to an early pathological stereotyped pattern of interpersonal experience, the acceptance of which determined survival and reward and the rejection of which would have been catastrophic, since the subject was dependent on his significant others who were the initiators of these pathological transactions. The representation of this historic relationship became a basic affect organizer and source of unconscious motivation. It obeyed an early survival instinct but, with the changes of time, had become an impediment to the freedom to pursue happiness.

In the third part of the book, we put our theory into practice. Along with other clinical material, we use Freud's well-known and amply studied case of the Wolf Man to illustrate both the clinical foundations of the theory and the clinical application of the derived technology. In addition, we try to clarify the application of our model through examples of therapeutic strategy and technique.

On the basis of our observations, we divide therapeutic problems into two types. The first type, traditional to dynamic therapy, deals both with distortions in the passage to consciousness of unconscious material that is already a part of the subject's system of understanding, feeling, and acting and with the compulsive organization of unconscious motivation. The object is to release the patient from his compulsion and to restore the possibility of choice. This requires a symbolic reorganization. A second type of therapeutic problem deals with deficits and absences. It focuses on what needs to be learned and what is not yet signified within the constricted conscious-unconscious system. As a result of his historic experience within his family and his culture, these enriching representations and the experience that they represent are outside and dissonant to the organization that the person has given to his understanding. The patient is seriously handicapped in his healthy efforts to find happiness because the representations to which we refer have not yet been identified and incorporated into what the person perceives as significant. While they are absent, they are essential to solve vital problems. For example, the immigrant who is making an adaptation to a new culture must incorporate significant dissonant concepts and meanings held by and valid in the community in which he is now residing. The same is true in life crises when the task or the conditions for its fulfillment change dramatically.

This second issue, the expansion and enrichment of the constricted conscious and unconscious spaces, becomes significant in completing the therapeutic task of transforming the vicious circle of the compulsive repetition of pathology into an open spiral of creative learning. Freeing the subject to go somewhat beyond his constricting preconscious assumptions, to overcome rigidity and impermeability and enrich his actual understanding, is the key to our form of psychoanalysis. As he becomes free to go beyond these assumptions, his motivation is liberated from his unconscious compulsion; his affects are enriched and cover a wider gamut of feelings, and the conscious and unconscious spaces find a new more encompassing structure. Moreover, the desire itself must be freed from certain historic and cultural limitations. To fulfill the new and enriched desire for happiness, the client must resolve the tendency to use interpersonal power sadomasochistically in a blaming and devaluing defense. He must have control over, or access to, the politicoeconomic resources necessary for his projects for self-fulfillment. We have elaborated the importance of interpersonal and socioeconomic power in a previous book, *Patients and Agents* (Gear, Liendo, and Scott 1983).

For the process of improving the quality of symbolic and actual life, we distinguish between and treat distinctly the deficits, defenses, and resistances that impede the therapeutic process. In our schema, deficits are found on the conceptual, emotional, and operational levels. If desire is to be fulfilled, these deficits must be compensated or corrected by the incorporation of new understandings, feelings and skills and by a new social setting. Defenses are raised against traumatic anxiety; they produce a displacement from the relevant dramatic, creative, and productive tasks that must be undertaken to gain happiness. Instead, the subject occupies himself with the task of unfairly distributing devaluation and blame to others—a process he identifies as the "solution" to resolve his state of anxiety. The anxiety is taken as the problem itself, rather than as a sign of an underlying problem. In the resolution and working through of defenses, the traditional dynamic principles and techniques are applied. Resistance is defined as the force that acts against change; it is considered to have an affect and a social component. The social component is taken into account in the importance given in analysis to the reinforcing environment, which can impede or favor change.

We have reconsidered therapeutic techniques for overcoming affect resistances and for freeing desire from compulsion. We find that analysis of transference is not enough; a clearly designed and redefining therapeutic setting is also needed. We have concluded that unconscious motivation is reorganized only through the client's experience of living new patterns of relationships. This new experience represents the missing solution to the analysand's historic pathogenic paradoxes. The option that would resolve his paradox had not been signified within the constricted conscious or unconscious spaces. It is notably absent. The paradox is resolved by the design and living of the specifically corrective and enriching therapeutic experience and confirmed in the therapeutic environment. In this way, desire is released from the melodramatic compulsion, and affect is enriched.

The content of the unconscious is the traditional domain of psychoanalytic therapy. What lies outside the unconscious represents a new and enriching domain that we consider worthy of systematic consideration and inclusion in therapeutic work. The articulation of this domain to the symbolic system allows the development of a broader and genuinely changed understanding.

It is from the *extraframe* metaconscious space that the analysand makes a relatively objective analysis of personal assumptions and his social context. An analysis of these assumptions permits the development of greater flexibility and openness of communication between the potential unconscious space and the *intraframe* space, thus changing the subject's capacity to assimilate what is new and potentially relevant to his life. In this way, he can go beyond his stereotyped and impoverished melodrama to claim emotional competence and achieve the freedom necessary to gain happiness.

Just as psychic spaces have been realigned in new dimensions, so therapy has been recast. To the traditional depth dimension of *working through* the unconscious material, paradigmatic psychoanalysis has added the dimension of *breaking through* to the potential unconscious. On the clinical level, a metapsychological distinction can be drawn between the unconscious, which is based on material present but distorted, and the potential unconscious, based on material which, although clinically notably absent, is indirectly deducible because the missing representations are necessary for a symbolic resolution of the dramatic task. Their absence produces observable failures. These two types of clinical observation correspond respectively to what is signified, in the former case, within the preconscious frame and to what lies beyond the preconscious frame, in the latter case, in the potential unconscious. On the therapeutic level, these two types correspond to the distinction between working through signified material and breaking through by way of frame analysis to the potential material.

Our intention in writing this book has been to conserve and enrich Freud's fundamental theories, actualizing and modifying them with our contribution. We believe that there is nothing more practical than a good theory and hope we have illustrated this in our application of paradigmatic psychoanalysis to clinical material and to therapeutic technique.

We have proposed a new pentadimensional topical theory that considers five psychic spaces: the constricted conscious, the actual unconscious (superficial and deep), the framing preconscious, the potential unconscious, and the metaconscious.

A new classification of clinical material is derived from the topology: excessively present, infrequently present, unquestionable, notably absent, and material about material. The melodramatic theme of interpersonal mistreatment is present in a striking manner in that it is reiterated continually. The dramatic problem of a vital failure, usually socioeconomic, is infrequently commented upon because attention has been defensively displaced to the melodramatic defense. The socially shared assumptions are taken as natural and unquestionable. The solution to the historic dilemma is notably absent, often being repudiated because it is dissonant to the value and cognitive frame assumptions. Material about material refers to comments on a metatheoretical level about the thought process and the implicit assumptions that organize the material.

The new theory and organization of clinical material determines new objectives and new therapeutic stages. These include: control of emotional incompetence, working through of the melodrama, working out of the dramatic incompetence, breaking through of the constricting frame, enrichment from the potential unconscious, the mutation of the pathogenic environment, and the design and implementation of a new project for happiness.

1.

THE WOLF MAN: CASE ILLUSTRATION

We will illustrate the application of our theoretical model both with our own clinical material and with one of Freud's best-known cases, that of the Wolf Man, beginning by giving a brief summary of the history of this case. It was presented by Freud in "From the History of an Infantile Neurosis" (1918), where he focused in his analysis of the Wolf Man on the infantile phobias, which appeared when the Wolf Man was three years old, and his compulsion neurosis, which developed at the age of ten.

At the time of his first analysis, at age twenty-three, the Wolf Man was suffering a severe incapacitation that had lasted for five years and had occasioned treatment in various sanatoria. He had been treated by Krae- pelin before visiting Freud. Later, he was treated by Ruth Mack Bruns- wick at Freud's request, when he became very hypochondriacal and devel- oped symptoms that Mack Brunswick describes as "paranoid" (Gardiner 1971). Finally, he was befriended by Muriel Gardiner, who helped him to prepare his extensive autobiography and served as his counselor. In his later years, he was also treated by other analysts, in treatments that took place after the Russian Revolution, in very changed economic circum- stances and after he was forced to make his home permanently outside Russia. In his last years, the Wolf Man was interviewed about his life and illness by a journalist, Karen Obholzer, who published much of this material upon his death (Obholzer 1982). The book contains a wealth of direct quotations. Thus we have an opportunity to explore information about the Wolf Man from a variety of sources—both indirectly, as he was understood by others, and directly, from recorded interviews and his

writings about himself—while he was under various analysts' treatment
in totally different circumstances over a period of years. A synthesis of the
case follows, based on information from these different sources at different stages of his life and treatment.

IDENTIFYING DATA

When he entered his first analysis, the Wolf Man was a twenty-three-year-
old Russian-born aristocrat, son of a landed gentleman who was an
honorary judge and active in politics. At the time of consultation, he was
the only living child, his sister and father both being dead, his sister from
suicide. He had a secondary-school education in an exclusive private
school and depended totally on his inheritance for his income, an inheritance to be administered by his mother until he reached the age of twenty-
eight. The Wolf Man first consulted Freud in Vienna, where he was
visiting, after he had had a difference with Kraeplin, his attending physician, who had recommended that he not marry Therese, a lower-class
foreigner nurse, whom the Wolf Man had met in the sanatorium and who
had been his nurse there.

GENERAL MANNER AND APPEARANCE

Dressed extravagantly, as befitted a Russian aristocrat, the Wolf Man was
accompanied by his personal valet and his private physician. He gave
Freud the impression of complete dependence.

PRESENTING COMPLAINT

The Wolf Man consulted Freud because of a social and emotional incapacity that he related in his mind to the development of gonorrhea when he
was eighteen. He had considered himself "favored by fortune," but this
superstitious belief had been dramatically and undeniably disconfirmed by
the misfortune of the illness.

He was completely dependent on others and did not take care of his
own needs even in the most minimal way. Freud stated that "his shrinking

from self-sufficient existence was so great as to outweigh all the vexations of his illness" (1918: 11).

HISTORY OF ILLNESS

The Wolf Man's history of psychological problems dated back to infancy. He underwent a dramatic change in character at the age of three and a half, when he became, according to Freud, "irritable and violent" (1918: 15). The associated "traumas" identified in treatment by Freud were a seduction by his sister, at an early age supposedly seeing his parents having sexual relations, and being under the care of a very cruel English governess who attacked and mistreated his "Nanya" (nanny).

His only sister committed suicide as a young woman. Two years his senior, she had been a precocious, active, and intelligent child and had easily surpassed him in all fields. Completely unlike the Wolf Man, she was particularly studious and uninterested in the frivolous things of life. In addition, she particularly delighted in his fear reactions. When he was young, she repeatedly showed him pictures of a wolf, to which he reacted with great distress and fear. Her death brought conflicting emotions: on one level, according to his analyst, the Wolf Man was pleased with the increase in his inheritance; on another, he gave an account of having become depressed by the loss.

Nanya, his dedicated nanny, was the one who raised and taught him more than anyone else. She is described by Freud as a simple, loving, rigidly religious person who had lost a child of her own and, as a result, dedicated herself to the Wolf Man.

Freud notes the Wolf Man's compulsive choice of love objects, always from the lower class. At the time of the first consultation with Freud, the Wolf Man had developed gonorrhea in an affair with a servant girl. In later years, he married Therese in spite of Kraepelin's recommendation to the contrary. In the last twenty years of his life, after Therese's death, he took a woman of very low class as a lover.

The Wolf Man's father had been a manic-depressive and had required hospitalization on various occasions during the Wolf Man's growing-up years. He died when the patient was twenty-one.

His mother was a severe hypochondriac, who spent little time with the patient in his infancy. In spite of her many complaints, she lived to the age of eighty. She was left to administer the family fortune after her husband's death, since he did not trust the judgment of his only son. The Wolf Man blamed and devalued her after his father's death in his attempts to obtain more money from her, although he recognized that she had been fair in her handling of the family fortune. She continued to permit him to live without responsibility until he reached the age to administer his fortune.

The Wolf Man had grown up in prerevolutionary Russia in a position of economic power and privilege. He had been educated in a gymnasium and had returned to the university after his marriage to Therese, obtaining his university degree with his wife's encouragement. During his adult years, he suffered the effects of the Revolution, losing his family estates and much of the inherited fortune. This reversal caused him to migrate permanently to Vienna and created the need for him to work or somehow to meet his economic requirements as well as the additional responsibilities of caring for his mother and his Nanya. A friend found him a job; Therese encouraged him to stay with it.

The Wolf Man perceived other people as frightening, and his dreams and memories of his infancy included nightmares in which he was persecuted and terrified by animals—wolves, giant caterpillars, and snails—and in which he was paralyzed with fear and helplessness. In his infancy, he was known to have tortured animals and to have been quite an irritable child from the age of three.

The most famous of the Wolf Man's dreams occurred when he was four years old. He was lying in his bed in what he identified as the wintertime, when a window swung open. He was terrified to see six or seven white wolves sitting motionless in a walnut tree. The wolves, which looked like sheep or sheep dogs, were paying attention to something. The most impressive element in the dream was a sense of motionlessness. The Wolf Man spoke of screaming in terror of being eaten by the wolves, and he awakened to be consoled by his Nanya.

In his analysis, Freud concluded that the dream represented the Wolf Man's castration fears, which resulted from seeing his parents have "coitus a tergo," three times. The Wolf Man could never recall this event, however, and in later life seemed unconvinced of its occurrence. He seemed rather unhappy with the technique of dream interpretation, in which the therapist stated the meaning, in contrast to analysis of free associations, in which he could participate more actively in the conclusions. The associations used in the interpretation were related to fairy tales—"Little Red

Riding-Hood," "The Wolf and the Seven Little Goats," "The Wolf and the Tailor."

This dream, the analysis of which influenced the history of psychonalysis so strongly, will be reexamined within the theoretical framework of this book. We will give a new organization to the meaning of the facts, but of course we will limit ourselves to the information provided in this richly reported case.

In his narrative and his behavior, the Wolf Man constantly blamed others—his mother, his sister, Freud—for frightening him or for trying to cheat him by trying to take his money, although he actually took money unfairly from them.

THERAPEUTIC EVOLUTION

When Feud set limits on the Wolf Man's transferential dependence, the analysis took a decisive turn. Freud fixed an arbitrary date of termination, at which time, regardless of his condition, the Wolf Man would be on his own. This action by Freud produced a noteworthy and dramatic improvement. The Wolf Man terminated his analysis and returned to Russia. He married Therese, his lover for the past seven years, and began to study law at the University of Petersburg, where he succeeded in graduating, at the age of twenty-eight, when he also achieved economic independence from his mother.

Again, just before the Russian Revolution, Freud treated the Wolf Man for "transference residuals." This treatment took place when Therese left him temporarily to attend to her dying daughter. After the revolution, the Wolf Man required treatment again, and this time, because Freud had fallen ill with cancer and because of a very difficult transference resistance, Mack Brunswick treated him. She believes that the Wolf Man's transference resistance to Freud's therapeutic efforts was not resolved in part because Freud was collecting money to help him. According to Mack Brunswick (Gardiner 1971), the Wolf Man was hiding information from Freud about the family jewels, which he had managed to remove from Russia. He had persisted in a transference resistance and was also acting out his repetition compulsion with Freud.

Mack Brunswick found the Wolf Man manipulative and seductive; he compared her with Freud and others in the hope of becoming her "favored son." She seems to have taken a much firmer and more nonpreferential attitude toward him, refusing to be seduced by comparisons with Freud and encouraging him to seek work. The Wolf Man was able to achieve economic independence and to care for dependent members of his family as a result of treatment with Mack Brunswick. A position was found for him as a clerk in an insurance agency.

The Wolf Man became very well known as a result of the treatment with Freud. With the help of Muriel Gardiner, he succeeded in writing an autobiography (Gardiner 1971). After Therese's death by suicide, his later years seem to have been characterized by an association with Luise, a psychopathic and exploiting woman whom he described as a "slut." Paradoxically, the outcome that both his father and Therese had predicted and had tried to prevent occurred in his relationship with Luise: in Freud's terms, there was a "return of the repressed."

I

AN EXPANDED TOPOLOGY

2.

WORKING WITH THE
POTENTIAL UNCONSCIOUS

We will here explore a model consisting of five psychic spaces: the constricted conscious, the actual unconscious, the preconscious frame, the potential unconscious, and the metaconscious. The preconscious is seen as a frame which divides the psychic spaces into those that are *intraframe* and those that are *extraframe* (Figure 1). Within the frame, organized and delimited by it, are the traditional conscious and unconscious on which classical psychoanalysis focuses as it undertakes the task of making conscious the material already present but repressed in the unconscious. Outside the preconscious frame are two newly defined spaces: the metaconscious and the potential unconscious. In the potential unconscious are representations that are specifically absent from the conscious and unconscious and are essential to the resolution of the analysand's historic and current problems. Their absence is clearly evident to the analyst because they are the missing pieces of a symbolic puzzle. They are essential to the freeing of desire from the repetition compulsion and to the analysand's ability to pursue happiness.

A central problem of therapy thus becomes the inclusion and articulation of this absent but essential material. Another important task is an analysis of the assumptions that give meaning to the analysand's experience. This paradigmatic analysis allows the subject a kind of "break through" that opens him to a greater symbolic potential. The therapeutic model is termed "paradigmatic psychoanalysis" to emphasize that an analysis of the person's preconscious informal theory of relations to self, others, and the

17

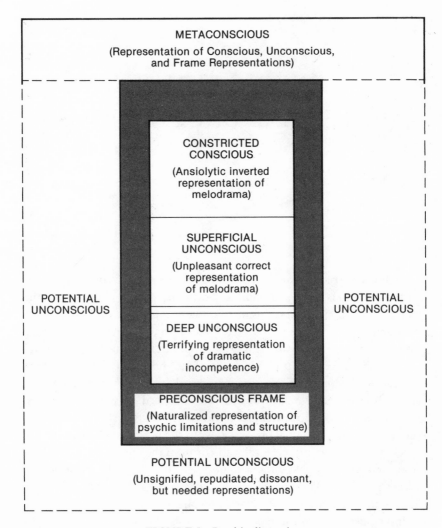

FIGURE 1. Psychic dimensions

world is essential to the opening of the *intraframe* psychic spaces and to the *freeing* of desire from the repetition compulsion.

The Closing of the American Mind, claims that the American college student's lack of a sense of history has made him too open and indiscriminate, having no clear context to give to his thoughts and experiences and no congruent system of convictions. It is our experience that this lack of understanding of the historic, social, and personal context of learning does not produce a true openness so much as intellectual impoverishment and incongruence in beliefs. A free and open person has convictions that he understands within a context and can critically examine. We believe that an awareness of assumptions, values, and personal and social history is essential to the development of an understanding of how we understand, feel, and act. This awareness of the context in which we have developed our superego, the set of givens with a strong affect charge, enables us to avoid dogmatism. If a contextualizing analytic perception is absent, the superego becomes a dogmatic legislator, rigidly perpetuating the law. A truly free and open person is not indiscriminatingly open. The model presented here readdresses the liberating function of psychoanalysis as it frees people to pursue their own symbolic and affect enrichment.

FREUD'S FIRST TOPICAL MODEL

Using the case of the Wolf Man and other clinical material as illustrations, we offer a detailed analysis of Freud's widely known metapsychological topical model (1915). We will do this for three reasons. First, because the model represents assumptions known to or shared by the reader, it provides a common base for examining and understanding new concepts from widely diverse origins, which form a part of the conceptual frame for this book. Second, Freud anticipates remarkably well the questions considered relevant for current consideration, questions that are readdressed from a distinct frame of reference here. Finally, an examination of Freud's model implies an analysis of Freud's preconscious frame assumptions. We will attempt a logical analysis of certain discoveries made analogically and intuitively by Freud in his clinical work with patients. That is, we will analyze the personal and social context of Freud's thinking as well as his conclusions.

In his first topical model (1900), Freud divided the psychic apparatus into three parts, which he called the unconscious, preconscious, and conscious systems. The basis that he used for this division was accessibility to consciousness. The material that was not available to consciousness, except in special circumstances and with difficulty, was grouped together as the unconscious. The preconscious system included elements readily accessible to consciousness when attention was directed to them. Conscious elements made up the conscious system.

Each of these systems—and their systemic nature was emphasized by

Freud—had other distinguishing characteristics in addition to accessibility to consciousness. Freud originally thought that the unconscious was limited to "primarily repressed" thing representations, although he later recognized the existence of "secondarily repressed" verbal material as well. He characterized the unconscious as using primary process, by the nonverbal nature of its memory traces, and later as operating under the pleasure principle, by its relation to instinctual life. Freud attributed the motive force of mental energy to sexual impulses residing in the unconscious, and he assumed additionally that its nonverbal nature favored the perpetuation of childhood wishes, dreams, and fantasies.

Freud believed that the preconscious, unlike the unconscious, was not present form birth but rather developed from childhood to adulthood. He assumed (1900) that the unconscious normally had access to consciousness through the preconscious, which gives labels to its nonverbal elements. The preconscious could deny access to consciousness of the unconscious material; that is, it could exercise censorship, resulting in repression. This process occurred chiefly in relation to the system of moral standards and value qualifications that was assumed to reside there. Freud also thought that the preconscious, like the conscious system, shared the same secondary-process and reality principles.

INFORMATION: REPRESSED OR UNARTICULATED

Implicit in Freud's position is the idea that if the material in the unconscious could pass the preconscious barrier, it would become a part of the conscious system. Therefore, treatment emphasized the passage of information from the unconscious to the conscious.

It became clear to us that accessibility to consciousness was distinct from incorporation into the structured understanding given to consciousness by the organizing and delimiting preconscious paradigm, which converts "raw data" into *meaningful* information (Bruner 1973). The preconscious frame, or paradigm, has a personal moral and attitudinal aspect, which makes what is articulated a part of it, emotionally charged with a degree of conviction. (The word "paradigm" has various meanings. Kuhn (1970) defines it as an informal set of assumptions shared by the scientific community. Barthes (1967) would give it a syntactic function as an organizing instrument that gives the "grammar" to structural relations. It is also a system of assumptions that are affectively charged. The strength of affect is one factor in the paradigm's resistance to change. The term will be used in this book as implying all three meanings.)

Freud himself notes that there is a "distinction between that which emerges as a perception and that which *belongs* to the conscious system" (1918: 586). In his metapsychological model and in his understanding of the process of cure, Freud does not seem to attribute great importance to this distinction between being perceived as belonging and simply being recognized.

In contrast, we place great importance on the incorporation of emerging perceptions into the preconscious-conscious systems in the process of cure. It is a principal task in the practice of paradigmatic psychoanalysis (Gear, Liendo, and Scott 1988). The material dissonant to the organizing frame is neither repressed defensively nor present in the unconscious; rather, it lies *outside* the limits of the preconscious assumptions in what is defined here as the *extraframe* potential unconscious. This material is specifically and notably absent from the analysand's speech, though, again, it is apparent to the therapist because the assumption of its presence is logical. For example, a paranoid patient perceives others as either deceitful or deceived. There is a notable absence in his speech of any reference to trustworthy and supporting relations, although such relations are necessary to live happily. The lack of trust may be made conscious fairly readily, but effective incorporation of the idea of trustworthiness into the psychic system is resisted because: (1) the material is dissonant to the frame assumptions; (2) it may not be shared by the general community of significant others; (3) it must replace habitual patterns of behavior; (4) attempts to act upon it entail learning a whole series of new and complex operational procedures.

The problem of overcoming preconscious-frame resistances to change and working with the potential unconscious becomes a principal focus of psychotherapy based on this new paradigm. While the openness sought is not indiscriminate, emphasis is placed on increasing the breadth of the constricted conscious space and on the resistances and defenses against the *inclusion* of the dissonant information from the potential unconscious.

When in conflict, the Wolf Man, like the majority of our patients, was not free to consider ways to achieve happiness. What he perceived and understood at such times involved the distribution of whatever displeasure already existed. He had become threatened by an overwhelming anxiety which made him return to the historic problems of who was to blame or who was inferior. In the analytic material this abusive type of

relationship was present in the constant repetition of his theme of mistreatment. He assumed that the world is organized by themes of superiority and inferiority, entitlement and exploitation. These assumptions
predetermined his compulsive concern with *how* he was being slighted,
cheated, or mistreated. This constricted view left in the potential unconscious any idea that his treatment could be fair. To confirm his assumptions, he sought to interact in an unfair way with an "inferior" being. If
one were to point out his unquestioned stereotyped relation of mistreatment, he would take it as natural, as the only possible relation between
people. As we can see, it would not be difficult to make him aware of the
relation that he established. What would be difficult would be to introduce alternate ways of relating.

Obviously, the Wolf Man must have experienced cooperative equal
relationships, but these were not incorporated into his symbolic system.
He did not consider them natural, and the values and behaviors they
entailed did not motivate him. His speech, rather, gives innumerable
examples of what he considered natural behavior and appropriate motivational factors: his perception of himself as used, cheated, mistreated,
and exploited—by Freud, by his mother, and by Luise, his lover for the
last twenty years of his life. This material is not only present in the
evidence from the various sources, it is strikingly and excessively so,
although in a distorted form involving an inversion of perception between
what is identified as the self and what as the other. The Wolf Man
identified himself as mistreated, while he mistreated the other.

In the terrible and interminable relationship with Luise, as the Wolf
Man described it to Obholzer (1982), he still continued, sixty years after
his first analysis, in this melodramatic theme of how he was being exploited, cheated, and mistreated by an inferior being. Luise shared his
game, considering the mutual mistreatment a natural form of behavior in
which she justified herself by stating, "He had exploited people, so why
not exploit him in turn?" (Obholzer 1982:188).

One does not doubt that the game was a real game of mistreatment.
The questions are why the Wolf Man played this game compulsively for
more than sixty years, and why he had so much difficulty in developing
an interest in games of mutual support or productive endeavors. The
Wolf Man's speech specifically lacks references to mutually beneficial and
enriching interpersonal partnerships, built on the assumption of a relationship of equality of worth. We consider these possibilities to have been
beyond the limits of his fundamental assumptions. They were present in

his potential unconscious, and although they may have emerged into consciousness if his attention had been called to them or as a result of creative, playful thinking, they were neither integrated nor truly understood. They were not *meaningful* in that they were not a part of his personal theory about his relations to self, others, or the world. Nor were they motivating because they were not articulated to his unconscious affect organization, which functions within the limits of what is articulated.

The problem of change is not resolved simply by providing information (Watzlawick 1978). Neither dynamic insight nor an awareness of deficiencies is followed automatically by a change in behavior. Such information must be incorporated into basic understanding and action systems. In the Wolf Man, as in all of us, change is resisted. In his case, he resisted because the new information was: (1) morally and cognitively dissonant; (2) not personally motivating; (3) not shared by others, such as Luise; (4) did not represent the habitual behavior of many years of reinforced, unhealthy habits; (5) new behaviors were difficult to learn without taking risks and investing time and effort. Therapeutic procedures must take all these factors into account. Interpretation is a therapeutic instrument specifically useful in making the unconscious conscious. Other instruments are required to approach the task of articulating and integrating representations present in the potential unconscious (Horowitz 1977; Kolb 1984; McCarthey 1980). For example, it would not have been enough to interpret the Wolf Man's fear of inferiority. He would have had to learn new skills to develop competence. In such situations the therapist must help to select a milieu in which mutual respect and valuing is the prevailing attitude and in which the patient will be encouraged in his efforts at independence.

THE PENTADIMENSIONAL MODEL AND ANALYTIC MATERIAL

Our distinction between *intraframe* and *extraframe* allows a clear therapeutic focus on the difference between problems of repression and problems of articulation and integration of *extraframe* material into the system. Repressed material is present and signified in the unconscious, being absent from consciousness or present in a distorted form. In the conscious clinical material, there is a stereotyped, reiterative, and distorted content in which the analysand is preoccupied with and reenacts a theme of interpersonal blame or inferiority in which he perceives the other as doing what he is doing. This material is classified as excessively present. In the deep unconscious are the affect organizers of the symbolic system, including the traumatic representation of what is most feared. This is indirectly present in the clinical material and can be deduced from the analysis of dreams and free associations. Notably absent from the material but present in the *extraframe* potential unconscious is the representation of mutually respectful interpersonal treatment. What is absent may fairly readily emerge as a perception. It is difficult, however to integrate the perception and to give it significance in the conscious and unconscious systems.

The frame determines both the limits of the constricted conscious space and the structure of its content. That is, it determines the syntactic relations of this constricted space. The frame establishes logical categories and determines the relations possible among them. The manner in which this is done further reduces the information available for resolving personal and social problems. Universal syntactic errors include oversimplification and the organization of categories into bipolar opposites. We define these errors as universal deficits because they tend to appear consistently and globally in the logical organization given to thought.

Within his defensive and restrictive game of distributing displeasure unfairly, the Wolf Man perceived others in a simplistic way: they were either "cheaters" or "cheated," "exploiters" or "exploited." Information that did not fit into these categories was lost to the subject in his problem-solving efforts. In addition, within this constricted definition of the problem and of the available roles and actions, the choices that the Wolf Man could make posed a fundamental dilemma (Whitehead and Russell 1910): he would either have to exploit others or be exploited by others. There was no other option represented. The solution of a fair, constructive, cooperative relationship among persons of equal human worth did not occur to him; it was *extraframe*. Information about this essential but absent material is registered by the therapist in the same way that Sherlock Holmes was able to solve the mystery of "The Hound of Baskervilles," by noting a very apparent "absence." The hound had not barked as would have been expected.

The following clinical example will clarify the difference between material that is present and evident in the constricted conscious space or is repressed in the superficial or deep unconscious and the material that remains in the potential unconscious, represented but unsignified.

Peter came to consultation at the insistence of his wife, who had been his college sweetheart and to whom he had been married for many years. Before their marriage, their relationship had been very intense: they had studied together every day and were together every evening. Later, they practiced the same profession but worked in different companies. His wife described herself as being intensely dedicated to the relationship. Now, however, Peter wanted a divorce. The couple has two children, age nine and eleven. Since the birth of the first child, Peter has been unfaithful to his wife. For the last four years, he has had a lover, who is divorced and is a very bright and ambitious woman. As a child, Peter was abandoned by his father. His mother had to care for his younger brother, who was severely ill with asthma. He recalls his sadness and sense of not being loved or important since his mother gave her undivided attention to his sick brother.

In a session, Peter described his relationship with his lover in the following way:

"She is there, intensely absorbed in me. I feel like the center of her universe, even if for fleeting stolen moments. Then comes the loneliness. I go back to my wife, and I feel unattended. She bustles around. I know that it is for the children, but it makes me feel very bad."

In the relationship with the therapist, Peter would ask for sessions and then come late or, at times, not at all. When this was pointed out to him, he rationalized, saying that work kept him from coming. During joint sessions with his wife, Peter expected to be the center of discussion and would become distant and not participate when attention centered on his wife. He was abandoning of his wife, therapist, and children although he perceived himself as abandoned.

In Peter's constricted conscious space was the direct perception and representation of himself as an abandoned child, unattended and unimportant. Repressed in his superficial unconscious was his own tendency to abandon, as is evident from his own actions with his wife and children. On a deep level, his motivating affect was organized in two categories, represented and affectively signified as positive "absorbing relationships" and negative "abandoning relationships." His extramarital love relationship functions because the time that he can spend with his lover is limited by the nature of the relationship. It would likely fail as a marriage because of Peter's intense self-absorption and unrealistic demands. His lover has told him that she does not want a marriage to him because he is so absorbing. He is unable to resolve the problem of abandonment because the solution of a mature 'shared life together is not available to him. Furthermore, he is neither able nor motivated to develop a truly sharing relationship. This absent representation is apparent to the therapist as an essential element for the solution of problems and the overcoming of the repetition compulsion.

In his potential unconscious, unarticulated to his paradigm and affectively unsignified, is the representation of a mature relationship in which togetherness is achieved symbolically through sharing of interests. When he entered treatment togetherness was confused with possessiveness. By "affectively unsignified" we mean that such a relationship has no emotional meaning and therefore is not motivating. It is not linked to the deep unconscious affect organizers. What, because of its essential nature, should have been symbolized was not. It appeared to the therapist as a notable absence.

What we term "notable absence" was dealt with by Freud when he used the term *verwerfung* in his case of the Wolf Man to refer to what is repudiated by the subject; in the Wolf Man's case, according to Freud, the reality of castration. In his analysis, Freud recognized that, although *represented* at the age of one and a half, the primal scene witnessed by the Wolf Man at that age was not signified until he was much older and able to give meaning to it. One may recall personal experiences or comments that were not understood in infancy but, with the accumulation of experience, could later be given meaning. Sexual jokes and comments are often heard and remembered by a child, even though they are not understood. These experiences are represented, or they could not be recalled. However, they have no emotional significance until later in life.

Lacan (1966) took Freud's idea of repudiation and developed it in his description of foreclosure, which is differentiated from repression in two aspects. First, the foreclosed signifiers are not integrated into the subject's unconscious. Second, they do not return from within, as does repressed material, but from "outside," from the real. "Foreclosure" refers to some fundamental signifier (such as the phallus as a signifier of castration) that has been left out of the symbolic world. Its absence is notable because of its essential role in an effective symbolic system. Lacan related the mechanism to the development of psychosis.

We would agree with the proposition that certain essential signifiers are missing from the conscious and unconscious symbolic space and that these symbols have the characteristics described by Lacan. They are essential in dealing with the real world. They are not repressed; they are absent.

Their return is related to their being essential for the subject to address the life problems that otherwise go unsolved as a result of their absence. They could be said to provoke the return of the repudiated, from without, from the real world, as opposed to the return of the repressed, from within. We would not, however, limit this phenomenon to psychosis. It is universally encountered. Since there is no representation of an essential symbol, this failure will be detected as a notable absence of something essential to the subject every time he comes in contact with certain problems in the real world. In other words, what is absent makes itself palpably present when the subject repeatedly fails to resolve a historic dilemma or a vital problem.

We relate these absences to preconscious organizing assumptions that give meaning to experience and actively select out—repudiate—experience that is dissonant to the moral and cognitive assumptions. Our experience is that the most habitually selected out material from the analysand's symbolic world tends to be related to structures of power, both interpersonal and socioeconomic (Gear, Liendo, and Scott 1983). The absences in this symbolic system produce an incompetence that guarantees a return of the repudiated. The subject is unable to overcome his traumatic fear of vital failure because his symbolic system has left the solution of these problems in the potential unconscious, which lies beyond the preconscious constrictions.

We consider introducing and dealing with the absent material essential to successful treatment. We therefore give more than a theoretical consideration to the problem. Thus, preconscious frame analysis and frame resistance to the inclusion of absent but vital material is a key consideration in this book.

INTRAFRAME DRAMA AND MELODRAMA

Following Freud, the constricted *intraframe* space can also be divided into the conscious and unconscious spaces. The thought process of each is distinct. Unconscious activity is characteristically analogic and associative, while the conscious uses a process that is principally verbal, digital, and logical. When we examine the contents of the Wolf Man's conscious space, we find, especially in moments of conflict, a tendency to limit conscious content to an irrelevant melodrama of mistreatment rather than to identify the feelings and problems provoked by the real dramas in his

love and his work. As we have said before, he consciously perceived and
spoke of interpersonal unfairness, cheating, and exploitation, always from
the position of the victim (Gear and Liendo 1975). In contrast to the
absent dramatic theme, the melodramatic theme of mistreatment is strikingly present in his speech and actions.

The Wolf Man's unconscious content was equally stereotyped. He
tended to dream of destructive attacks. We would place the direct representation of self as exploiting and cheating in his superficial unconscious.
This representation was repressed from consciousness and identified projectively in the other, who was seen consciously and consistently as the
victimizer, the cheater, or exploiter. Absent from the *intraframe* spaces
were representations of cooperative, constructive relationships dedicated
to mutual support and understanding and concerned with the production
of happiness rather than the distribution of unhappiness. This was the
Wolf Man's melodrama.

For us "melodrama" refers to a compulsive tendency to reiterate in
speech and action a stereotyped relation of mistreatment characterized by
interpersonal blaming or devaluing. The roles in this melodrama are
perceived inversely to how they are being acted; for example, the mistreating victimizer sees himself as mistreated. Since there are four general
abusive relationships possible—those of being blamed or blaming and
those of being devalued or devaluing—there are four roles in the melodramatic defense. Those who actively blame or devalue others are defined
as sadists, while those who are blamed and devalued are defined as maso-
chists. The four roles are: the sadistic devaluer, the sadistic blamer, the
masochistic devalued, and the masochistic blamed.

The following case illustrates the melodramatic defense of a masochistic and devalued patient.

Diane is thirty years old. She was referred by a colleague for treatment
of an acute depression precipitated by her husband's abandoning her for
what he perceived as a more active and optimistic woman. He is a
successful and brilliant academician, although rather impatient and incon-
siderate. He complained that Diane was incurably pessimistic, very "than-
atic" (morbid) and that she had finally defeated him, since he now considers her incurable. Diane claimed that her husband had abandoned her
not because of her pessimism but because she was very stupid. This she
affirmed clearly and in a very alert, intelligent fashion.

Diane is a very attractive woman who appears much younger than her
age. However, she perceives herself as appearing old and unpleasant. She

and her husband have two children, aged four and six. She feels unable to educate them and feels that she is going to impede their development. There are no objective signs that this is the case. The children are progressing normally in school and have an excellent relationship with their mother. Her parents are living, and she has two siblings who are "successfully married." She began, and then abandoned, several university careers because she was sure that she would not be able to practice them professionally. She had not sought psychotherapy before since she was sure that she would not be able to derive benefit from treatment because of her lack of intelligence.

In her sessions, Diane compulsively exercised the same melodramatic routine in which she took the role of the person "realistically pessimistic and failing," assigning to the analyst the role of "the reassuring utopian optimist." After entering the session with a gesture of overwhelming resignation, she associated on the couch in a very able manner about how she is incompetent to resolve her problems with her husband, children, parents, and so forth. The therapist concluded that she exaggerates her incompetence since her discourse demonstrated a basically good relation with her children and her parents. She has developed a relationship with another man who is a competent and successful professional. Although very much in love with her, he is subtly demoralized by her constant self-devaluation. The analyst perceived Diane as treating herself very unjustly. His first impulse was to convince her that she is not a poor partner, daughter, or mother. She had, in fact, finished a course and received a diploma in special education during the year that she had remained in treatment.

Diane induced a countertransferential response in which the other tries to inject enthusiasm into her while she objects with a series of "Yes, but . . . ," implying that the analyst either falsly praises her or, more often, that he acts as an incurable optimist. She would tell him, "You see me better than I am," or "You don't want to understand just how stupid and useless I am." When the analyst would not accept these affirmations and would point out her objective performance as a mother, a daughter, or a partner, she would reply, "Yes, but it is not easy," or "It won't last," or "I'm only good for trying to patch up my messes and to cover up my stupidity as best I can." The analyst eventually showed her that she has chosen this particular theme because it is self-denigrating and induces in the therapist the role of compulsively attempting to offer her an optimistic view of life. He pointed out that treatment could easily turn into a blind repetition of the self-devaluing melodramatic escape from anxiety into a narcissistic dialogue between a "realistic pessimist," the patient, and a "utopian optimist," the therapist. In this case, she would be compulsively repeating the mother-father relationship in which her mother was an enthusiastic but unrealistic optimist and her father was a pessimistic and embittered failure.

Her father did not limit himself merely to discouraging and embittering his wife. He actively sabotaged any constructive project that she initiated. This was also the case with the relationship between Diane acting as her father and the analyst perceved as the mother. Not only did Diane induce the analyst to attempt to encourage her in an optimistic fashion, she also sabotaged treatment by doing such things as not wanting to accept a sufficient number of weekly sessions saying that she did not have the resources. In fact, she counted on the support of a very affluent husband and his family who wanted her to be happy. When, at last, she agreed to a sufficient number of sessions, she began to arrive late or neglected to come, claiming that she had forgotten, was too busy, and so forth. In this way, she converted her own organizing assumption "It is not so simple" into a reality. The therapist had to struggle with his own sense of defeat and demoralization as he felt the emotion induced by Diane's defeatism. At these moments, it seemed possible only to drain her of emotion but not to modify it since there was no lived insight and no elaboration. Therapy was confined to the *intraframe* conflict.

It was only by the analyst's constant awareness of Diane's repetitive melodramatic theme that he could overcome the effect of her sense of failure and provide conditions for truly helping her to understand, resolve, and overcome the self-perpetuating melodramatic escape. Her husband's abandonment had precipitated a need for change in response to a loss of protection. Her competent husband who had taken over disappeared.

The therapist first had to escape from the entrapment in the role of the optimistic mother. He then had to help Diane to define the real dramatic problems resulting from her husband's abandonment and make clear that her perception of the problem was what made it insoluble. The therapeutic relationship had to be redefined as did the problem of how she perceived the problem. At the same time, her active sabotaging of the therapeutic efforts had to be confronted. Her tendency to perceive, talk, and act in the role of her father had to meet with a response that was more than the naive optimism of the mother. That is, the therapist had to introduce from the potential unconscious the representations that were necessary for solution: a perception of herself as competent and the establishment of the missing category of "realistic optimist."

Diane's complaint that she was congenitally and incurably stupid had some base in reality in that she had been so masochistically self-devaluing that she had remained undeveloped both intellectually and emotionally. As a result of her lack of experience, she did not have much capacity for attention, concentration, and tolerance for anxiety, and this made problem-solving genuinely difficult. Instead of seeking help for her problem, she simply labeled it "insoluble." In this way, she affirmed that she was unintelligent and avoided the anxiety of persisting in the effort to improve her abilities. She was intelligent but a defeatist.

Diane refused efforts to improve her general cultural level or to become deeply involved in any professional issue. She sought all types of excuses and rationalizations when these were prescribed for her. She used many ways to avoid the task at hand, often with some activity that made her so busy that she could not continue with the real task, protesting that to try was just more evidence of stupidity. She justified her lack of persistence in many ways and resisted both its recognition and its correction.

It was necessary to pressure and to "oblige" her to use her intelligence and to stick with a task. Fortunately, this objective was gradually achieved.

This woman had been reluctant to try what she already perceived herself as unable to do. She had refused to dance at her wedding because she felt unable to dance well and did not want to look foolish. Of course, she looked foolish for refusing. Her husband had initially accepted her reluctance to learn, but he finally lost interest and called her "my little dumb rib" and abandoned her in boredom and defeat.

This is what the analyst attempted to avoid in treatment: that the analysand provoke exactly what she feared, as Freud indicated in 1914. He would have summarized the therapeutic work into "Tell me what you fear, and I will tell you what you provoke. I will also show you how to avoid this provocation and how to avoid inducing a complementary role in the other." In Diane's deep unconscious is a fear of failure and stupidity that is defended against by her denying her competence to learn and refusing to try. The melodrama appears when she avoids recognition of a dramatic problem. A dramatic problem is defined as producing a threat of a vital failure as a result of some symbolic, affect, instrumental, or biological deficit.

DRAMA AND THE PROBLEM SPACE

The dimensions of the space in which any subject addresses a vital problem (Newell and Simon 1972) is defined by his framing assumptions. When the solution lies beyond the constrictions of this space, the problem cannot be solved. This space must be examined for how it is constricted and oversimplified, how it creates dilemmas, and how it is distorted by inversions in the perception of identity of self and other. We hold as a general rule that people under stress tend to identify a melodrama rather than the dramatic problem that is producing the threat of a vital failure. A woman facing divorce is likely to feel failure as a woman. When death occurs, the dramatic situation tends to be overshadowed by a melodrama of who is to blame, and the dramatic loss and its implications are not addressed. In such cases, people perceive the problem defensively as if it were one of self-worth or guilt. In addition, because of the organization given by their constricting frame to the melodrama, people oversimplify their classification even further of expected human characteristics into two polar opposites: people are either good or bad, superior or inferior. Neither alternative gives a viable solution. Moreover, because of the tendency to project defensively, they see the other as playing the role that they actually play in the stereotyped and irrelevant script (Gear and Liendo 1981a).

Diane sees relationships as consisting of optimists who are foolishly unrealistic and the pessimists who see things clearly but hopelessly. The category of an optimistic realist did not exist for her; it is missing in her symbolic system.

THE POTENTIAL SPACE AND SELF CONCEPT

To emphasize further the important distinction that we make between the *intraframe* and the *extraframe* spaces, we present a similar concept put forth by Winnicott (1971; Ogden 1985). He identified a "potential space" between what he considered to be clearly "self" and what is identified as clearly "not self." We could say that, in his view, information exists that is not articulated to the self but, at the same time, is not totally foreign or strange to it. For Winnicott, such representations form a potential space, in which both analytic and creative, or playful, thought are a part. In our model, we identify two distinct *extraframe* spaces in accordance with the distinct coding mode and the characteristically distinct functions of each sphere. The digital mode, which is analytic and is the above dimension, forms one space; the other is formed by the analogic mode, which has creative functions and lies beyond the frame constrictions, our potential unconscious. *Above* is used here to define a distinct level—the metalevel—the content of which refers to the other levels. The metaspace is outside and above the framing assumptions of the paradigm. We argue that certain important material is identified projectively in the other and seen as not self, being a repressed unconscious part of the intrapsychic system. We consider that it is very important to maintain the distinction between what is present but repressed and what is totally absent from the organization given to the symbolic system. Therefore, we organize our model in terms of the concept of a selective, structuring, and delimiting preconscious frame and not in terms of the distinction between self and not self. Therapeutic techniques are different for dealing with what is present, but distorted or repressed, and what is totally absent.

The frame resistance to mutation is related to its degree of permeability and rigidity. We identify two mechanisms involved in this resistance: a dogmatic mechanism in which what is valued is idealized and what challenges values is denigrated out of hand; and a cognitive resistance in which what is believed is taken as natural, as the only thing *possible* to believe (Glauser 1978). Frame resistances are also markedly enhanced by the social and shared nature of the assumptions. Those who continue to share the assumptions of the group are rewarded. Those who change them are punished socially. Since beliefs are shared and acted upon, those who conform obtain a pragmatic confirmation (Cicourel 1973). An example will help clarify the concept.

Within the constrictions of her paradigm, Diane had the notion of the inevitability of defeat. Pessimism was a part of her "self." She was impervious to the suggestion that she was a capable woman and that she was in fact a successful mother. She perceived any lack of success as natural, attributing it to her innate and incurable stupidity. Her thesis about herself was shared by her father, and her husband came to believe and share it as well. Her own lack of trying tended to make her pessimism realistic as she managed to create conditions for defeat. Her problem was that she lacked the emotional competence to deal with the anxiety that would have been produced by a consistent effort to face inevitable setbacks, continuing to try until she improved. She preferred the uncomfortable anxiety of feeling stupid to the overwhelming anxiety that she felt when she tried to face the task to be learned.

The *extraframe* space, as we have defined it, helps to broaden the tasks of therapy. Enrichment from the potential unconscious becomes a new therapeutic task. Development of the *extraframe* spaces becomes clearly important since therapeutic technique depends on the existence of a well-developed analytic (Viderman 1970) and potential space (Winnicott 1971). Attention to the boundary between *intraframe* and *extraframe* spaces provides a base for strategic and tactical decisions in therapy. The *extraframe* spaces are linked clearly to therapeutic strategic tasks. Certain material that has remained in the potential unconscious must be integrated into the subject's understanding, if he is to resolve his historic dilemma. For example, Peter must include the idea of sharing and personal autonomy in his understanding of what it is to love. He must also recognize his own abandoning behavior, which although already signified within the frame, is repressed in the superficial layers of the unconscious. Diane must include a realistic optimism within the possible attitudes. Unconsciously she has an *intraframe* repressed representation of herself as one who defeats others while she consciously sees herself as defeated. The treatment implications of this *intraframe* and *extraframe* distinction will be elaborated in detail in Part III.

3.

THE DELIMITING
AND STRUCTURING
PRECONSCIOUS FRAME

The preconscious frame serves the necessary and healthy function of organizing information into understanding. It forms a boundary between the *extraframe* metaconscious and potential unconscious spaces and *intraframe* conscious and unconscious spaces. The preconscious frame maintains the subject's ability to explain, predict, and anticipate environmental events and to prepare for action. In terms of game theory, the preconscious contains the assumptions that determine the individual's social and personal script. From it are derived the lower-order rules and roles with which this script is played out. It structures the general paradigm of understanding, which, because it tends to resist change, can give continuity to understanding and permit the subject to anticipate and prepare for a future not too dissimilar to the past.

It will be noted that we are placing in the preconscious what cognitive theorists would call the structure that transforms "information into understanding" (Bruner 1973). This structure is not placed in the unconscious because it is not deep or conflicted; rather, it is encompassing and organizing. In the dynamic sense, no defense is involved when the preconscious structure and assumptions are made conscious. Although easily made conscious, they strongly resist change. Simply making the assumption conscious obviously does not produce any dissonance in the psychic system. When they undergo detailed examination, however, and when they are challenged on the level of their correspondence to reality and relevance and effectiveness in daily living, the subject experiences great anxiety. If he faces a major failure of his theory, he will suffer a state of inner chaos or, at the least, great confusion. Therefore, the subject will raise a defense against the anxiety produced by a challenge to his frame assumptions. He will try to avoid the recognition of the failure and will resist change.

This phenomenon is illustrated in the case of the Wolf Man, who was faced with a pragmatic challenge to a fundamental frame assumption that precipitated his illness and first caused him to seek Freud's help. According to Freud, the Wolf Man had been totally conscious of an important frame conviction: a belief that he was privileged and protected by a special circumstance of birth. The Wolf Man did not question this belief; he took it as natural. The dramatic *failure* of the credibility of his framing assumption (Festinger 1975) produced the overwhelming anxiety and resulted in an exaggerated state of fear and dependence. Freud says:

> It was not until just before taking leave of treatment that he remembered having been told that he was born with a caul. He had for that reason always looked upon himself as a special child of fortune to whom no ill could befall. He did not lose that conviction until he was forced to realize that his gonorrhoeal infection constituted a serious injury to his body. The blow to his narcissism was too much for him and he collapsed. (1918: 580)

What precipitated the crisis was the anxiety provoked by the undeniable failure of one of his fundamental assumptions. We have witnessed this phenomenon in our clinical experience in countries in which an economic collapse has taken place. The protected and highly privileged children of the upper middle class are terribly disturbed when they find that their assumption that they have been born to live an easy life is suddenly challenged. Similarly, most therapists have had experience with immigrants suffering from culture shock in which their beliefs and theories are no longer shared and their performance does not produce the expected result.

FRAME ACCESIBILITY FROM WITHIN AND FROM WITHOUT

The preconscious frame is accessible to consciousness in varying degrees. It may be conscious, but qualified as natural and therefore unquestioned. In this case, the judgment is made from inside the frame assumptions, and the frame, although accessible to consciousness, is still judged from within. It may, however, be accessible to consciousness by way of an *extraframe* analysis. In this case, the frame itself is evaluated in terms of its valuative and cognitive constrictions and in terms of the adequacy of the frame for the tasks necessary to fulfill desire (i.e., correspondence and relevance). Valuative and cognitive assumptions are identified and analyzed; when they are found not to be pertinent to the present environment, they must be enriched and made relevant.

Like his father, the Wolf Man regarded his privileged protection as natural and did not question it until a dramatic failure forced him to do so. He assumed that Freud would sustain him economically by making an annual collection for him from among his friends, and he allowed himself to be kept in this dependent state long after he had found work (Brim and Stanton, 1966). He considered this idea to be natural and rationalized it as something Freud wanted to do. He did not evaluate his assumptions critically but took them as unshakable truths. He did not, in other words, question privileged protection but rationalized about it from within the assumption that it was natural.

Likewise, Peter functioned in terms of preconscions frame assumptions. He assumed that any love relationship was exclusive and possessive. In his rationalizations, he disqualified his wife as cold and indifferent when she looked after the children, and he believed that his possessiveness was natural and expected. And, in a similar fashion, Diane thought that feelings of failure were natural and inevitable, rationalizing them as being the result of her stupidity.

CONSTRICTING NARROWNESS

The frame must, of course, be in some sense narrow in that it is impossible to include all potential events or explanations in a given theory: every theory has finite dimensions (Kuhn 1970). The narrowness of the preconscious frame, however, must be distinguished from a pathological resistance to change of the concepts within it. A simple frame narrowness becomes actively constricting as a result of its impermeability and rigidity. The narrow mind is unchangeable as well as narrow. Although limited, a healthy mind is more open to the incorporation of new material whenever the pardigm fails. In the healthy individual, a significant failure brings a reevaluation of assumptions.

We propose that, in important ways, frame "permeability-impermeability" and "flexibility-rigidity" are two distinct concepts (Rokeach 1960). In healthy subjects, the degree of permeability is related to the "expected" or the "needed" (Bruner 1947). Unexpected material, dissonant to the frame and not needed, is selected out of conscious attention. Attention is simply not given to it. Although it may be registered and represented in consciousness, it remains located in the potential unconscious. It is given no value or emotional significance. Diane, for example, did not attend to the evidence that she is a successful mother, while Peter did not attend to the evidence that it is possible to love without possessing.

At times, what is perceived as lacking significance is precisely what is vital to mental health. The Wolf Man, for example, was impervious to experiences in which he was loved and respected, receiving a fair compensation in accord with his contribution (Lerner 1975). This absent perception was essential to his mental health. In such a case, the absence must be corrected, such correction being a part of the *extraframe* tasks of paradigmatic psychoanalysis.

To be given meaning, of course, this material must first be noticed, which occurs after a relevant event is repeated persistently (redundance). After many recurrent episodes, what was originally taken as chance or exceptional is finally regarded as somehow significant. In terms of communication theory (Abramson 1966), the dissonant passes from noise to information.

When the Wolf Man visited Therese and found her in a deteriorated physical state (she suffered a severe depression as the result of her decision to separate from him), he was affected by the discovery that she loved him for himself, not for his economic power. The evidence was finally irrefutable. She did not know that he would come. She was obviously depressed as a result of the separation. To have come to this state, she must truly have loved him. He had thereby identified and confirmed the information that he himself was lovable. It had passed from meaningless noise to highly motivating information. As a result, he decided to marry Therese in spite of the pressure of his mother and his society.

Diane was able to confirm the unbelievable: that she was intelligent. This was achieved, in part, by constantly pointing out that she had passed her course, was successful as a mother, and so forth, and by the analyst's interpretations that she used her self-representation as stupid to escape her anxiety about failure, a view that justified her giving up before even trying. When she finally recognized that she was not stupid, information that had been registered as meaningless became meaningful.

A certain degree of impermeability is present even in healthy people. Without it, the subject would be paralyzed by constant attempts to develop new meaning in relation to nonsignificant variations (noise). This state of excessive plasticity is what Bloom (1987) describes as the pathologically open mind. It is found in those "as if" personalities that constantly change with minor variations in their surroundings. A much more common problem in psychotherapy is the opposite: pathological rigidity. Individuals in this condition do not change the preconscious frame itself even in the face of clearly significant and repeated failures in their ability to explain the world (Wason 1968). Freud writes the following about his treatment of the Wolf Man, in which he noted first an impermeability to the meaning of what was being said and then a rigid resistance to change, even after the message was understood.

> The patient with whom I am here concerned remained for a time unassailably entrenched behind an attitude of obliging apathy. He listened, understood and remained unapproachable. His unimpeachable intelligence was, as it were, cut off. (411)

With impermeability, the information is heard and yet it has no real meaning. It must be heard repeatedly before it is incorporated into the system of understanding. Here Freud recognized implicitly that interpretation is not enough; therapy is an ongoing process of re-education, in which the frame resistances are as important as the unconscious defense. To be complete, the interpretation must include reference to the specifically "absent" material that must be recognized, learned, and put into practice. The interpretation must include what is needed to solve the problem, as Freud recognizes:

> It took a long education to induce him to take an independent share in the work; and when as a result of this exertion he began for the first time to feel relief, he immediately knocked off work to avoid any further changes, and in order to remain comfortably in the situation which had been thus established. (477)

The patient rigidly resisted change. Even after he understood the information, he did not want to suffer the anxiety of change. To change is a process requiring an investment of effort far beyond the use of intellect.

DOGMATIZATION BY IDEALIZATION
AND DENIGRATION

Rigidity, as we have stated, depends on two types of mechanisms: valuative and cognitive. The valuative frame defense consists of a dogmatic attitude about what has been shared socially and culturally. That is, the analysand uses defensive splitting (Klein 1975) and idealizes his social and cultural framework while denigrating any other possible framework. Thus, what is valuatively dissonant is denigrated and qualified as bad or inferior, while what is valuatively consonant is idealized and qualified as good and superior. The qualifying evaluation is made from within the frame assumptions themselves; it is the mechanism by which the frame defends against the anxiety of a need for a mutation.

The Wolf Man confirmed his idealization of the Russian aristocratic value system and his denigration of other systems with the following comments:

> My father said he was not worried about me. I had healthy tastes. I went hunting, horseback riding, etc. (Obholzer 1982:46)
>
> How could I have introduced Therese there? . . . That she didn't speak Russian would have been the least of it. But that she didn't speak French was much more serious. In Russia a girl had to know French. (44)
>
> They always preach that women, that the common people, are human beings just like those who belong to the educated class, that another point of view is prejudice. (75)
>
> Aristocrat, that was the class, the class was entered in the passport. Dvorjanin. And grazhdanin was ordinary citizen. (75)

To speak French, to be aristocratic, to ride horseback, were idealized, whereas being like Therese, practical and concretely helpful, was denigrated.

Peter idealized a state of mutual absorption. He overvalued the fleeting but intense attention of his lover while denigrating his wife's independent contribution to the well-being of the children and her economic contribution to the family.

TAKING ASSUMPTIONS AS NATURAL

The individual derives his "ideology," including his attitudes toward social class, from the assumptions shared by his society. But these cognitive assumptions may be taken as natural, as "the way things really are" and not simply as one of many ways to understanding experience. This process curtails the search of the potential unconscious. The subject is not aware that he could seek another possibility. Also, incoming dissonant information may be distorted and significant difference not registered. As a result of distortion, the subject perceives the information as consonant with and confirming of the assumptions. Diane saw failure as natural. She failed to seek, or even to attend to, evidence of success. Since she could imagine no outcome other than failure, she did not struggle. She had learned a state of helplessness that was self-confirming and self-perpetuating. She distorted information about success, registering it as evidence of failure.

The Wolf Man's state of privilege was so natural for him that its termination was inconceivable to him, or even to others around him, like his father. The Wolf Man took note of his father's assumption when he commented:

> When I was twenty or twenty-two my mother wrote that my father was planning to teach me the rudiments of farming. It's a little late when you are twenty-two. And then my father died. . . . All these things would have interested me, but my father didn't bother with any of them. He thought there is enough money and there always will be. No need to concern oneself with practical matters, with the running of the estate. (Obholzer 1982:89)

The Wolf Man also rationalized the importance of the annual collection that Freud took up for him, saying that the collection was not taken regularly and that the family jewels he had managed to rescue were not really valuable. He continued to rationalize, saying that he had not withheld information about this, and that after all, as Mack Brunswick relates (Gardiner 1971), Freud knew that he was working but continued to make collections. He then went to accuse Mack Brunswick, saying that her observation was false and a personal attack. In this example of a defensive personalization, the Wolf Man escaped totally from examination of a relevant problem, his economic dependence (Gear, Liendo, and Scott 1983). He replaced this drama with his attention to the interpersonal melodrama of victimization.

Diane assumed her own state of incompetence. She rationalized it as an inevitable result of her stupidity. She defensively reduced her arguments to a personal level, disqualifying the analyst when he tried to encourage her, likening him to her mistaken optimistic mother whose encouragement was foolishly unfounded. That is, she disqualified the analyst rather than looking at the evidence.

Peter rationalized his lack of a positive relationship with his wife. He personalized his arguments, qualifying her as cold and inattentive to him and accusing her of being the one who abandoned him and failed in her duty.

THE FAMILY NOVEL:
A VERSION OF THE SOCIAL GAME

Preconscious frame constrictions occur on two levels, the social and the personal. First, there is the constriction of a particular family game, played in the way characteristic of a society. The family novel is evident in the compulsive actions and speech of the analysand. It is an important part of his conscious and unconscious structure, appearing in dreams, free associations, and so forth. Thus, family experience determined the Wolf Man's need to play the game of superiority and entitlement as an aristocratic Russian. Privilege was related by society to birth. The Wolf Man's interpersonal game was structured around this aristocratic concern and played in the way of that culture at that time. As in the Wolf Man's case, such constriction limits the content of the *intraframe* conscious and unconscious spaces. Therefore, for the Wolf Man, interpersonal games were limited to "superiority and entitlement," played between a man identified as a superior aristocrat and a woman identified as an inferior "slut," or peasant. In Diane's case, the game was her own version of superiority-inferiority, in which she took the role of a stupid person and assigned to the other the role of intelligent one.

On the second level of the relationship between the *intraframe* conscious and the unconscious spaces, there are frame assumptions about the identity given to the self and other, which are learned from interpersonal relations with significant others. With his constant concern with superiority, the Wolf Man developed a stereotyed distribution of roles consonant with his assumptions about self and others. He routinely perceived himself as a superior victim receiving unfair and exploiting treatment, while perceiving the other in the complementary role of the inferior victimizer, exploiting him and treating him unfairly.

Therefore, it will be apparent on a clinical level that the Wolf Man always constricted himself to the game of "superior-inferior," played and defined in the manner of his society: "superior" is of privileged birth, well-mannered, and elegantly dressed in accordance with the social values. In addition, he always devalued the other: a slut like Luise, of inferior birth; unable to speak French like Therese. This game was consonant with his identity assumptions and role assignments. At the same time, his perception was inverted in relation to action. He remained powerless and dependent—a well-dressed clerk with an exceptional tailor—who said that Freud overestimated his own work (Obholzer 1982:33). Ironically, the Wolf Man whose only source of fame is that he was Freud's patient perceived Freud as overvaluing himself! This concept of defensive inversion has been elaborated in our prior publications and forms an important part of the theoretical framework of paradigmatic psychoanalysis (Gear and Liendo 1980).

THE DISTORTING, POLARIZING, AND OVERSIMPLIFYING STRUCTURE

In addition to being narrow and constricting, the preconscious frame organizes information in a second way: by polarizing, distorting, and oversimplifying. That is, the frame also has syntactic organizing functions —polarizing and causally simplifying—in relation to the contents of the constricted conscious problem-solving space.

On the level of organizing the categories with which the subject classifies his relations and his experience, the preconscious frame significantly alters the logical space. The syntactic structure given by the frame is often that of dyadic, mutually exclusive complementary categories. Stated algebraically, the categories are (a) : (−a). They do not include the universe of all logical possibilities represented in the logical formula as (a) : (not a) (Whitehead and Russell 1910). Concretely, mutilation of the logical possibilities divides the world of experience into simplistic polarities: victim-victimizer, superior-inferior, valuable-valueless. This division results in a significant loss of possibilities and important information. Failure becomes inevitable. For example, there is no category for recognizing and classifying those who don't play a victimizing game. Such representations remain in the potential unconscious. Their absence is evident to the therapist. They must be included if a subject such as the Wolf Man is to be free to solve the problems which keep him from happiness.

Diane defeated herself when she categorized people into realistic pessimists (a) or the opposite, utopian optimists (−a). All problems became discouraging and insoluble. For Diane, those who believed that they have a solution were foolish utopians who would be defeated if they struggled. Those who saw imminent defeat were discouraged realists who had no reason to struggle. The category of realistic optimists did not exist for her. She was, of course, discouraged and discouraging, giving up before really trying.

Causality is often attributed in a stereotyped way to the person who is the blamed or devalued member, whereas his partner is routinely exoneralized in its attributions (Piaget 1970a, 1970b). When Diane attributed the therapist's encouraging comments to an unrealistic and unfounded the therapist's encouraging comments to an unrealistic and unfounded optimism, she subjectively disqualified him. She reasoned that his innocence had caused him to believe that there is hope. When the Wolf Man attributed his economic plight to bad advice given by Freud and his banker, he was simplifying the situation and making it a personal problem. Hence, the person perceived as responsible is morally blamed.

A concrete example of the complementary inversion of identity between the two principal actors in the melodrama is evident in the Wolf Man's devaluation of Therese and her overvaluing of him. He shared with her the inverted perception that he was superior and she inferior:

> Freud said that I was looking for something inferior because she was only a nurse, although people thought highly of her in the sanatorium. Freud said that I had received something very good you see because she was a very decent person. (Obholzer 1982:104)

In her suicide note, Therese threw a clear light on her own implicit assumptions about the identity she gave to herself and assigns to others. She assumed that the Wolf Man was the important one and exhorted him to seek the advice of protective others. That is, she accepted his narcissism and dependence. She reflected his needs and desires rather than her own (Gear, Hill, and Liendo 1981). While identifying herself as unimportant, she assigned to him the role of importance and worth. She also saw him as dependent and assumed the role of protector. She wrote:

> Marry a decent woman and go to sister—(a nun)—and seek her advice and don't become attached to some slut because that could be the end of you. (Obholzer 1982:95)

The Wolf Man commented, "She had understood the important thing," his tendency to seek out inferior women (103).

Therese saw his melodrama clearly and could understand his compulsive behavior. However, she took her own role in the melodrama as quite natural. Her assumptions about herself as unimportant and worthless were not commented upon. Her attention, even when facing death, was focused on the Wolf Man.

THE REINFORCING ENVIRONMENT

Any shared theory—and the preconscious paradigm is a socially structured and shared set of assumptions—tends to be self-perpetuating. Others and the environment attend to, induce, and reward the actions that are commensurate with the shared understanding, whereas they ignore, block, and punish actions that disconfirm these shared assumptions (Glauser 1978). This process is an important source of resistance to change. Logically, both the environment and the significant others must be taken into consideration when developing a treatment strategy. Treatment, therefore, includes a conscious selection or structuring of a new environment that will attend to, induce, and reward a better understanding of interpersonal relations and will favor the fulfillment of the new conscious desire (Gear, Grinberg, and Liendo 1976). The therapeutic environment is structured to provide experience that, up to that time, had remained *extraframe*. It provides conditions necessary to learn and reinforce the representations that are notably absent from the analysand's symbolic world.

The Wolf Man lived with a small group that confirmed his social and financial superiority. Although he consulted the best and most reknown physicians of his time, including Freud and Kraepelin, it is quite probable that he looked upon them as employees whom he was important enough to hire and powerful enough to pay. When he sought out Freud, he was traveling with a personal physician and a student of medicine whose exclusive job was to give him injections and to serve as a third in Russian card games. They were servants and status symbols. In his reference to the Wolf Man, Jones describes his initial relationship with Freud as profoundly degrading: "He initiated the first hour of treatment with the offer to have rectal intercourse with Freud and then to defecate on his head" (1955:273).

Diane also made a great effort to construct a pathological reinforcing environment. She induced her husband to treat her as stupid. She managed to avoid socioeconomic reality and to remain undeveloped. Peter was willing to abandon his family, which, after the birth of his children, did not favor his melodramatic game. He was attempting to reestablish a situation in which the environment favored his compulsive acting out of an absorbing relationship.

A PRAGMATIC CHALLENGE TO FRAME ASSUMPTIONS

Freud (1918) attributed the dramatic improvement in the Wolf Man to the fixing of an arbitrary date for termination of treatment. In a sense, treatment had become a confirming milieu in which the Wolf Man lived his life protected from the need for making decisions and assuming responsibilities. He lived comfortably, felt very important, and received an inordinate amount of attention. Simply by free associating and re-counting his dreams and fantasies, the Wolf Man was fulfilling his responsibilities to his new father figure, Freud. He was in a situation of little anxiety in which he could not fail in what was expected of him.

When Freud fixed an arbitrary date of termination, he reframed treatment and put the Wolf Man in a dilemma. Freud created a situation in which the Wolf Man's choices were reduced to dealing with his anxieties while accompanied by Freud or dealing with them after he was forced to leave the protection of treatment. Either way, he had to deal with his anxieties. There was no way to remain in a supportive therapeutic environment while putting off confronting the dramatic problems. The Wolf Man could no longer use treatment as a defensive pastime. Freud had managed to force the Wolf Man out of using treatment as a part of his system for confirming his assumptions and to place him squarely in reality. Intellectualizing in a secure, protective environment was one thing; getting well was another. Freud stated:

> The treatment must be brought to an end at a particular fixed date, no matter how far it had advanced. I was resolved to keep to that date; and eventually the patient came to see that I was in earnest. Under the inexora-ble pressure of this fixed limit his resistance and his fixation to the illness gave way. (1918:11)

In Diane's case, the therapist's insistence on conditions for therapeutic success dealt a blow to her self-defeating unconscious sabotage. Her frame assumptions received the pragmatic challenge of the therapist's response.

In summary, the delimiting and structuring aspects of the frame produce narrow and stereotyped interpretations of relations to self and others. These limitations are taken as natural and their modification is resisted by mechanisms of idealization and denigration. In treatment, the limitations may be challenged verbally or pragmatically.

4.

THE CONSTRICTED CONSCIOUS
SPACE AND PROBLEM-SOLVING

In this study, the constricted conscious space is defined as corresponding roughly to the space in which ego functions operate. It is related closely to the problem space as defined by cognitive theorists (Newell and Simon 1972).

This space is both limited and organized by the preconscious assumptions. Therefore, in pathology, it is constricted and oversimplified and often causally personalized and moralized. For example, Diane's logical space for problem-solving was very limited by her emotionally charged conviction that problems were insoluble because she was stupid and condemned to failure. Since she didn't try, with time her actual level of incompetence increased. The dilemma that impeded her had become "If I try, I fail and will show how stupid I am anyway. If I don't try, I fail and remain stupidly incompetent."

ERRONEOUS ASSUMPTIONS, LOGICALLY DEVELOPED

There are two levels of problem-solving thought, a level still within the *intraframe* conscious space and a level that analyzes the framing assumptions. The first level accepts the assumptions as natural and unquestionable. Within these accepted givens, it analyzes the logical structure of the thought process. It detects internal inconsistencies and rationalizations. Although it challenges the logic of the rules of the game, it does not challenge the level of the social definition of the game itself. While assuming the context, it deals with the logic of the content.

For example, given the assumption of the Wolf Man's father that society would always give the Wolf Man a privileged position, then his decision not to prepare the boy for anything except to assume the role of an aristocrat is logically consistent with the assumption. The father was concerned only with preventing the Wolf Man from squandering the family fortune on women of lower classes. In other words, he was limited in his maneuvers to tactical considerations. The strategy is already set. An examination of logical consistency is helpful in tactical decisions, but a strategic rethinking of a problem requires a meta-analysis of the assumptions. The frame becomes the focus of the analysis.

As we have said before, Diane assumed she would fail. Consistent with this assumption is the tactical rule "I'll quit before I fail." Tactically, in therapy she used her "stupidity" as a justification for not trying. Strategically, therapy had to challenge the assumption on which her tactics were based.

In healthy functioning, possibilities dissonant to the assumptions and generated in the potential unconscious are submitted to a conscious logical analysis. If they are useful in reconceptualizing or solving the problem and if they stand the test of reality, they are integrated into the preconscious paradigm. Healthy consciousness is directed at problem-solving functions. Possibilities are generated analogically and then tested logically against reality. Both the logical and analogical functions are necessary for the solution of problems and the fulfillment of desire (Bogen 1975).

The therapist worked with Diane to help her establish conditions for success. While he consistently pointed out her discouraging and discouraged assumptions, he also consistently pointed out objective evidence of success. He insisted on those conditions in therapy and in the general milieu that would permit real progress to occur and skills begin to develop. Thus he attempted to help her develop intelligent relationships in which she could experience a sense of personal worth and encouraged her to evaluate possibilities realistically. She learned to avoid excessive and unfounded optimism as well as the other extreme, paralyzing pessimism.

HEALTHY OPENNESS, UNHEALTHY CLOSURE

Health is related to a freer communication between the *intraframe* conscious space and the *extraframe* spaces, a communication favored by the resolution of defenses and resistances. In a healthy individual, the conscious space is inevitably narrow but not closed. New information may enrich the conscious space more readily than in the ill subject. It may be used to resolve new problems beyond the original constrictions.

In his careful evaluation of his own hypotheses, Freud displays his acute awareness of the necessity for openness and for logical evaluation of the creations of his potential unconscious such as the primal scene. His thinking is consistent and carefully elaborated as he examines the hypothetical construct of the primal scene. At the same time, he seems to have placed much more emphasis on the logical consistency of his hypotheses than on such factors as the probability of occurrence.

Freud demonstrates the importance that he attaches to openness and to the constant evaluation of formal or informal constructs when he states: "If I had not pursued my patient's analysis to the end, I would have been obliged to correct my *preconceived* opinion in a direction favorable to Adler. The conclusion of the analysis *unexpectedly* brought up new material that . . . enabled me to maintain my former conviction" (1918:22).

In pathology, the conscious space is made impermeable in relation to the potential unconscious by dogmatization—that is, by denigration of the valuatively dissonant and idealization of the valuatively consonant. Furthermore, a cognitive mechanism disqualifies the cognitively dissonant as "unnatural" or, alternatively, it may select out or distort incoming data so that it is perceived as if it were consonant. Taking what is expected as natural limits the search for solutions to the cognitively and valuatively consonant options.

Peter thus took both intensely absorbing and abandoning relationships as natural. He dogmatically idealized a symbiotic relationship and disqualified any other kind of togetherness. Since he could not conceptualize another alternative, he limited his search for a solution to his unhappy marriage to either returning to an absorbing relationship with his wife or divorcing her. He was already repeating the same type of relationship with his lover as he invaded her life, upset her personal plans, and made increasingly exclusive demands on her time.

THE INVERTED, OVERSIMPLIFIED, AND POLARIZED PROBLEM SPACE

We have already mentioned the *intraframe* defense against the passage of repressed material from the unconscious to the conscious space. As a result of this defensive inversion, what is valuatively and cognitively consonant with assumptions about self is identified introjectively in the self, whereas what is dissonant is identified projectively in the representation of the other. The dissonant is identified clearly as not of the self. This means that the roles in the melodramatic interpersonal sadomasochistic game are perceived in reverse to the way they are acted (Gear, Hill, and Liendo 1981). Peter perceived himself as abandoned while he acted in an abandoning way. He identified his wife as abandoning while she was, in fact, abandoned, as was the therapist.

Examples of inversion abound. An examination of the indirect material reported by the Wolf Man's analysts, the direct material reported by the Wolf Man himself, and of his actions as observed by others illustrates and reveals this inversion in the perception of the identity. For example, the Wolf Man stated that neither Freud nor his father were sufficiently aware of the socioeconomic situation in Russia, although he was the one who left Russia six months before the Revolution without making any arrangements to protect his fortune. He accused his mother of being unfair in her administration of the money, although she was actually generous to him (Freud 1918:550). The Wolf Man was being unfair to her while he perceived her as being unfair to him. He also inverted his perception of Freud. "I called Freud a scoundrel in my sessions of free associations." (Obholzer 1982:33). The Wolf Man's own behavior seemed to lack a healthy intention. Note, for example, his relations with women, his mother, and Freud.

The frame is also a structuring and organizing element that furnishes the tools for thought, for the categories of thought and their logical relationships. Here again, it has a causally simplifying and polarizing effect on what is available for the solution of problems.

Causal oversimplification manifests itself routinely in two ways. First, it is evident in the interpersonal blaming of one person by another, in which the problem and its causes are simply attributed to personal badness. Second, a narcissistic punctuation is given to the stereotyped transactions (Watzlawick, Weakland, and Fisch 1974). They are consistently perceived as originating with the self-blaming, masochistic member. As a result, the sadistic, blaming member qualifies and perceives himself as the moral victim of the other who starts the fight. In this way, the masochist suffers both moral and hedonistic displeasure. He distributes displeasure unfairly and does not contribute to efforts for happiness. We go so far as to define mental illness as characterized by concern with who is to blame or inferior. Productive concerns necessary for generating freedom and happiness are put aside. The undervalued masochist has accepted displeasure in exchange for the company of the overvalued sadistic other, who takes an unfair share of both hedonistic and moral pleasure.

While assuming no responsibility for leaving Russia hurriedly, the Wolf Man held Freud and a self-interested banker responsible for his dramatic economic loss. He had done nothing before leaving, except to take out some money in the form of a weak and devalued currency. He insisted that he did so at the recommendation of his "dishonest" banker. The banker was to blame; he was the victim. The Wolf Man had been away from Russia only a short time when he consulted Freud about whether he should return to Russia to save his fortune. In spite of this, he blamed Freud and held him totally responsible for his plight. Causality here is *simplistic, personalized,* and *moralistic.* Attention and action are directed toward the melodramatic blaming of others rather than toward solving a real and dramatic politicoeconomic problem.

Regarding the loss of his fortune, the Wolf Man stated:

> Reason told me: to . . . "Go there right now and settle your affairs." And I said to him "I would like to go because of my financial affairs." And he answered "No. Stay here; there is this and that to be resolved." And so I stayed. And that is why it became too late. (Obholzer 1982:48)

The Wolf Man acknowledged no personal responsibility in the decision. He assumed obedience toward the father-analyst as logical and natural. He perceived this important authoritarian assumption as shared and reinforced by the therapeutic setting, which, according to him, favored the transference neurosis. The Wolf Man did not grant importance to his own dependence, lack of interest in politics, assumptions about his privileged birth, and desire to be safe and comfortable in treatment. He simply blamed others.

In a similar fashion, Diane showed causal simplification when she always attributed failure to her stupidity.

TWO CATEGORIES: TWO FALSE CHOICES

The constricted conscious space is significantly altered as a result of the syntactic organization of categories into polar opposites. The options are reduced to two complementary possibilities, neither of which solves the problem. The result is a dilemma. If Diane, for example, was unrealistically optimistic, she became discouraged by the small difficulties she found in trying to complete any task. She gave up too quickly. If she was pessimistic, she simply gave up before even trying. In neither case did she persist until she could achieve success. The choice between unrealistic optimism and self defeating pessimism was a false choice that produced a "no win" dilemma.

For the Wolf Man, people were either superior, wise, unfailing, and omniscient or inferior, stupid, failing, and uninformed. He had to be omnipotent or impotent, victimizer or victim, totally responsible or totally irresponsible. He completely left out the possibility of a realistically responsible, mutually beneficial relationship between human beings of equal worth. It was beyond the limits of what he could imagine.

FITTING THE SPACE TO THE PROBLEM

Problems can be solved only in terms of what information is available for their solution and how this information is organized (Luchins and Luchins 1950). In our theory, the problem space and problem set are determined by the preconscious assumptions. Therapeutically, what is present but distorted must be corrected; what is not present but is essential to solution must be introduced from the potential unconscious. Notably absent material is not arbitrarily determined by the therapist. The problem that the analysand cannot resolve determines what is perceived as specifically absent from the *intraframe* spaces.

In therapy, problem-solving is analyzed on a specific and on a general level. Of course, the specific problems that the subject confronts must be resolved, but on a higher level of analysis, the person reviews the general procedures he uses in solving any problem (Newell and Simon 1972). The following steps are involved in such analysis:

1. The defensive inversion of identity between constricted conscious and unconscious spaces must be resolved.

Thus, the Wolf Man should have recognized that he projectively identified his inferiority in others. He should have perceived and corrected his own real inferiority by working on the skills necessary to be more effective, socially and economically. He wasted time and effort when he devalued others. In a similar way, Peter should be brought to stop blaming his wife for his emotional aloneness and to confront his own tendency to absorb and then abandon.

2. The frame assumptions should be analyzed on a metapsychological level, not taken as natural nor idealized dogmatically. Such analysis permits the entrance of dissonant information from the potential unconscious.

The Wolf Man's frame assumption of excessive and unfair entitlement should have been brought to his conscious attention. The game of superiority was part of an aristocratic social game shared by those in his original environment. He should have seen this concern as a limiting value judgment and questioned his own definition of superiority. That is, he should have perceived others, such as Freud and Therese, as truly valuable people. In addition, he should not have maintained his own self-esteem by associating with people like Luise, who by contrast, were socially his inferior.

Peter should be brought to see that abandonment and intense absorbtion are not "normal." He should understand the relationship with his wife as one of caring in the context of the demands of a family. He needs to understand that because she is caring, she is symbolically united to him even when occupied with everyday routine and the inevitable demands of job and family.

3. The conscious space should be expanded beyond its valuative and cognitive constrictions by integrating this information, which has entered consciousness from the potential unconscious.

Specifically, the Wolf Man should have experienced and integrated cooperative, fair, and productive games into his *constricted* conscious space. He should have identified those who share this orientation. In addition, he should have explored his potential unconscious, identifying options for developing real social power and abandoned the use of the defensive interpersonal "snob power" achieved by associating with people like Luise.

Peter should experience and integrate states of aloneness and distinguish them from emotional abandonment. He should seek out others who are cooperative and committed but not absorbing. He should begin to seek pleasure rather than simply trying to run from the historic displeasure induced by an abandoning father and a mother absorbed in others.

4. The newly enriched possibilities of the conscious space should be evaluated and analyzed (reality tested); new projects should be created and developed.

For the Wolf Man, such projects might have included studying law, writing his autobiography, or seeking the kind of interpersonal relations that produce happiness. He should have played with the creative ideas originating in his potential unconscious. The Wolf Man should have stopped games of mistreatment, stopped using another person as a depository for his inferiority feelings. He should have faced tasks that would have developed his potential and increased his self respect.

Peter should evaluate his marriage and his relations with his children and determine what can be modified and contribute to a better relation with his wife. He should enter into sharing activities.

5. The reality-tested enriching information found to be significant and relevant to the person's current problems should be integrated into the frame; that is, a new system of preconscious assumptions should be developed.

The Wolf Man should have replaced the assumption that he was helpless with a new set of assumptions. He should have given up his protector and gradually assumed responsibility. He should have faced and overcome his real ineffectiveness, rather than covering it up by seeking out an even more inferior woman whom he could then abuse and protect. Within the limits of these historic assumptions, his real potential for cooperative interdependence could not be developed. He needed to move from the motivation to distribute inevitable displeasure to a motivation to seek interpersonal and politicoeconomic pleasure. Specifically, the Wolf Man should have assumed and experienced a greater potential for social power: a more realistic self-image; a direct relationship between productivity and entitlement; a relationship between real security and a degree of independence and autonomy. *all these would feel to be N/M*

Peter should stop assuming indifference and abandonment when the other attends to personal or shared projects rather than attending to Peter. He should experience sharing and differentiate this from possessiveness. He should identify and face his great interpersonal insecurity. He should recognize the entitlement of the other. He should affirm that security in a relationship is related to giving respect and recognition to the other and accepting his individuality.

6. The problem should be addressed with the coding mode appropriate to the task: analogic possibility generating or digital reality testing.

In order to have achieved greater independence, the Wolf Man should have used his analogic capacity to imagine new projects, such as studies in his earlier years and writing his autobiography in his later years, directed toward increasing his real self-respect and toward producing happiness by increasing the capacity for socioeconomic achievement.

Happiness may be found when the person makes a symbolic reorganization and then applies this in the world of action.

Had he used his analogic capacity to generate new possibilities, the Wolf Man should then have evaluated them to make realistic plans for their achievement. He had difficulty in planning, often spending great amounts of time in the decision process because he harbored obsessive doubts and tended to avoid the frightening responsibility of his own decisions. His operational skills were almost all interpersonal, but even these were highly stereotyped. He showed an incapacity to identify his problems correctly, seeing the melodrama but failing to perceive the drama. He tended to convert the problems into something to be solved by submitting to an omniscient authority. Then he would leave total responsibility and planning to the other. When failure occurred, the Wolf Man would blame the other, personalize, and moralize, identifying himself again as the victim rather than analyzing and correcting his own inability to do something about the problems.

When the patient suffers high levels of anxiety, he limits efforts to solve problems more and more to what is already *intraframe*. Repeated failure results from: an inability to perceive and conceptualize the problem, the understanding of which requires that assumptions be challenged; a failure to generate an option for solution (the potential unconscious analogic thought is inadequate); or the inability to carry out the solution as conceived because of inadequate action skills or resources.

Diane's case shows the importance of developing new skills. She was ineffective, in part, because she did not have skills. To change her self-concept, she was strongly encouraged to develop herself.

In the face of rising anxiety, when failure occurs, the person regresses to the constrictions of his historic understanding. He becomes, literally, more narrow minded. His conscious space actually contracts, and he reenacts the interpersonal sadomasochistic melodrama. That is to say, he demonstrates a compulsion to repeat behavior determined by the historic affect organizers of the deep unconscious. When his level of anxiety is high, the subject demonstrates increasing impermeability and, most especially, rigidity.

When the Wolf Man's security was threatened, he conceptualized the problem incorrectly, as he had done historically, and submitted to a castrating and powerful figure. He did not see real and dramatic interpersonal and socioeconomic problems. Of, if he perceived them, he did not address them. His imagining was confined to variations on the theme of a castrated dependence and to a preoccupation with superiority-inferiority. Not seeing the problem, he could not develop new options for its solution.

Peter returned to the theory of his infancy: that he was a victim, abandoned by the father and uncared for by the mother. Having assumed this, he simply sought compulsively to be the center of the other's life.

When in crisis, the patient tends to think only within the assumptions of his interpersonal game of mistreatment. For example, when he suffered an important recognition of his socioeconomic castration, the Wolf Man defensively constricted his thinking *exclusively* to a sadomasochistic game: the interpersonal distribution of disagreeable feelings of inferiority and castration. The *intraframe* conscious problem-solving space was constricted severely. The Wolf Man's attention was occupied selectively by stereotyped interpersonal attacks of blaming or devaluing, which were excessively present in his speech and actions. He did not attend to the dramatic problem that precipitated his crisis; he infrequently referred to it in his speech. The solution to the dramatic problem had become less accessible to consciousness as the Wolf Man became more rigid and impermeable to the potential unconscious representations, *absent* from his speech and thought.

On a second level—being the first level the social and family restrictions on the game to be played—within this constricted game already defined by the preconscious frame, the analysand will be found always to assume the same identity, regardless of the real circumstances. That is, he identifies his own characteristics projectively in the other while introjecting the identity of the other. If given the chance, the Wolf Man would always have perceived himself in the role of the abused superior being and the other in the assigned complementary role of the abusing inferior person. He did this with Freud, Therese, Luise, and others. His actions were the opposite of what was consciously represented. He said that he was abused while he himself abused. In a similar way, Peter perceived himself as abandoned and neglected, when in reality he was actually abandoning and neglecting of his family.

In summary, problem-solving behavior addresses a strategic and a tactical aspect. The constricting preconscious assumptions are examined in the strategic aspect that deals with the opening of the *intraframe* spaces to enrichment from the potential unconscious material. The tactical level, while accepting the limitations placed on the space by the frame assumptions, is dedicated to developing new options for achieving the accepted goal.

Analysis of the problem-solving behavior of the analysand is done in a disciplined way both on the level of the specific problem to be solved and on that of general problem-solving behavior.

5.

THE UNCONSCIOUS:
SUPERFICIAL AND DEEP

The unconscious space contains constricted thought that is neither voli-
tional nor conscious; it is overdetermined. The organization of this unconscious thought is deducible from the analysis of "free associations,"
dreams and slips of the tongue (Freud 1900). Just as there is a constricted
intraframe conscious space, so the unconscious is stereotyped and constricted in its content.

This unconscious space is divisible into a superficial and deep part.
Among other representations, the superficial unconscious contains the
repressed analogic and digital representations of the melodramatic interpersonal sadomasochistic game present in an uninverted form. The representation corresponds with the patient's action. Direct passage of this
material to the conscious space is impeded by the preconscious paradigm
with its value assumptions and its assumptions about identity of self and
other. Passage occurs only after the distorting inversion has taken place.
In this way, the abusive sadistic subject avoids the anxiety of moral
dissonance, while the masochist avoids the threat to his survival, which
he fears would be the outcome of a challenge to the definition of relations
given by the sadist (Gear and Liendo 1981b). Both parties are trapped in
the victimizer-victimized definition of the relationship. It would seem
that, every time the analysand speaks, he tells the same story perceived in
reverse to how it is being acted.

Diane was the masochistic "victim" who devalued herself and induced
this devaluation on the part of others. She perceived herself as harmful to

her children and too stupid to be able to do anything well. She readily ceded the possibility of pleasure for the hope of survival under the protection of others more able to cope.

The melodramatic sadomasochistic game established by the Wolf Man consisted of two positions: he assumed that of a self-interested, blaming, devaluing, and exploiting victimizer and assigned to others that of a self-denying, overvaluing, and exploited victim. At the same time, his conscious portrayal of himself was inverted in relation to the enacted role. He described himself as the victim while behaving as a victimizer. We will now illustrate the Wolf Man's inverted perception of himself with descriptions of his behavior as recorded by others: that is, the inversion between the intraframe conscious and the unconscious representations.

He said, for example, "I called Freud a scoundrel. That sort of thing came into my head" (Obholzer 1982: 33). Yet in her description of the Wolf Man's actions, Mack Brunswick (Gardiner 1971:267) tells us that he was concealing information from Freud in order to continue receiving money from him—an unfair behavior befitting a "scoundrel." Although Freud found the Wolf Man's mother to be fair in her handling of the family fortune, the Wolf Man said accusingly "that she did not love him and that she was trying to economize at his expense" (Freud 1918:550).

The Wolf Man was devaluing in his treatment of others, although he was himself very sensitive to slights. He said about Freud: "He certainly wasn't very smart. He bought bonds from the Austrian government" (Obholzer 1982:45). The Wolf Man, however, committed just such an error when he left Russia. Or he said about women, "My wife Therese wasn't very intelligent either. . . . In any case there are very few intellectual women" (112). This, from a man who in fact was unable to reach his sister's intellectual level.

As Freud said: "I recognize the endeavour of the patient to debase his love object. This is to be explained as a reaction against pressure from the sister who was so much his superior" (1918:573).

The Wolf Man perceived others as selfish and self-interested, while he behaved in that way. For example, he said: "And again, the choice of Therese to be my wife. This was again to be a person below me socially. Or to be perfectly frank, either below me socially or out *for the money*" (Obholzer 1982:102). He perceived her as exploiting and selfish, while he described his own disinterest in her plight: "she told me that she had had a miscarriage. I had never concerned myself with such matters. That was stupid. It is something I should have thought about, shouldn't I?" (93). In contrast, Therese in her suicide note thought of nothing but his future and how to protect him.

The Wolf Man felt himself to be the victim, treated unfairly by his mother (handling of money); by Freud (loss of his fortune); by his sister (cruel and aggressive behavior); by Luise (accusing and exploiting). The representation in the unconscious, however, shows him in the opposite position: unfair, cruel, aggressive, accusing, and exploiting.

In such a situation, the inverted content is narrow and stereotyped. The representations are organized around bipolar "ego-alter" positions in which the action consists of someone taking unfair advantage of others. Not signified, but specifically necessary to health, is the representation of a relationship of mutual support and help with a fair distribution of benefits (Adams 1965). The articulation and integration of this representation will be shown to be necessary to enrich the affect organization of the deep unconscious. It is possible to release motivation from its melodramatic interpersonal compulsion only after this notably absent representation is signified and related to pleasurable affect.

In Peter's case, the affect-charged representations classified people into complementary classes, the "absorbing" and "abandoning". The experiencing of a mutually respectful togetherness must be identified and lived with a positive affect if it is to become motivating and desirable to Peter. For Diane, the categories were "realistic pessimist" and "foolish optimist." An attitude of optimistic realism was not recognized as such and was not affectively charged to become motivating.

In the melodramatic escape, the analysand tends to use seven preconscious and unconscious intrapsychic defense mechanisms in order to avoid being painfully aware of his incompetence. He escapes from painful lucidity to indolent limbo—"indolent" being taken in the double sense of passive and without pain. He not only escapes from drama to melodrama; he also inverts his perception of the sequence and direction of the mistreatment implicit in the sadomasochistic melodrama. These seven mechanisms are used simultaneously or sequentially, but always together. They are:

1. repression of dramatic incompetence;
2. displacement to the melodrama;
3. splitting of identities between victim and victimizer;
4. projective identification of one's own sadism (or masochism);

5. introjective identificatiion of the other's masochism (or sadism);
6. idealization of the victimizer perceived as a victim;
7. denigration of the victim perceived as a victimizer.

This block of defenses is effective in avoiding the traumatic anxiety but perpetuates the dramatic problem. There is an inevitable return of the repressed.

For example, a person who loses his job because he has not stayed abreast of scientific and technological developments tends to defend from the painful awareness of the true failure. He *represses* the perception of his progressive loss of skill and status and displaces his attention toward a problem of mistreatment with his wife. He *splits* melodramatic roles into those who mistreat and those who receive mistreatment. He begins to mistreat his wife and *identifies projectively* in her this mistreating attitude while *identifying introjectively* from her the identity of the one who is being mistreated. He then *idealizes* and overqualifies himself as a good, superior, and sensible husband, while he *denigrates* his wife, calling her inferior. These mechanisms limit themselves to a simple transitory neutralization of the psychic pain. Since they do not solve the underlying incompetence that produced the anxiety, there is a periodic return of the painful awareness of traumatic incompetence. In his moments of lucidity, the analysand lives a nightmare of anxiety.

Whenever the therapist notes the recurrence of this marked tendency to a sadomasochistic inverted description of what is happening, he must be alert to a crisis of incompetence. Every time the patient experiences a painful shock of reality, he represses the awareness of the real failure, displacing attention to the melodrama, to minimize displeasure when he cannot achieve pleasure.

The narcissistic escape is reinforced when the wife in the example acts as her husband's masochistic accomplice. They both believe that the problem is their relationship as a couple and fail to recognize the underlying problem of his incompetence. Their melodramatic manifest reason for the consultation masks a latent dramatic reason. If this definition is accepted by the therapist, he contributes to the perpetuation and aggravation of the failure. And if he treats the sadistic husband as a masochist and treats the wife erroneously as a sadist, he perpetuates the shared melodrama. The problem takes on an iatrogenic complication as the consultation further reinforces the seven defense mechanisms that the patient and his wife use unconsciously. Both the problem of sadomaso-

chism and the problem of incompetence must be confronted if a solution
is to be found.

DEEP UNCONSCIOUS COMPULSIVE DESIRE

On the deep level, of the unconscious are the affect organizers. Historically, a certain basic interpersonal relationship was bonded to a certain
affect. This relationship became responsible for the compulsive nature of
unconscious desire and for the strong convictions with which the subject
anticipates his most feared historic outcome. Paradoxically he contributes
unconsciously to assure that what he fears will happen. The breaking of
this interpersonal affect-experience unit represents the most commonly
protracted aspect of therapy. The strength of the affect on this level is an
extremely important source of resistance, as evidenced in the compulsive
motivation to repeat historic relations.

From the evidence of the Wolf Man's dreams, his history, and his
compulsive behavior, we would make the interpretation that his deep
unconscious contained the representation of a destructive, voracious "wolf
child" enraged by his father's unfair preference for his superior, talented,
and aggressive sister. This rage was terrifying to him because, if it were
expressed toward the more powerful father, there would be danger that
he would either destroy the father or be destroyed by his father, who
would be angered by his attacks. His rage threatened his survival.

Because of his own terror at the potential results of expressing any
aggression toward his more powerful father, the Wolf Man took an
unequivocally passive, socially castrated role. For survival, he became
dependent on the more active and superior other. His only way out of
this dilemma was to renounce the normal and essential degree of socioeconomic competitiveness and to become an increasingly more dependent
and frightened "inferior being," chronically in danger of abandonment or
attack. Paradoxically, his "solution" perpetuated the underlying problem.

In the logic of his deep unconscious, inferiority would be equal to
being helpless against the destructive attacks of others, while aggression
would be equal to psychotic destructive assaults on others. Therefore, fear
would be bonded to aggressive, assertive, and dominating behavior, necessary for socioeconomic development. For this reason, the problem of
inferiority and dependence *cannot* be resolved. If the subject attempts to
be assertive to overcome his inferiority, he feels the risk of attack. If he is

not assertive, he feels left out, unloved, and unfairly treated because of his inferiority.

The existential solution attempted by the Wolf Man was to be the helpless victim and to "find a good, protective woodsman" to save him from the wolves. He sought and selected a relationship with an inferior being who was not threatening and who, because of social inferiority or a need for money, would tolerate his degrading interpersonal outbursts of aggression without either reacting violently against him or abandoning him. At the same time, because she was inferior and economically dependent, this person did not frighten him. Thus, he could feel superior, valuable, and the center of attention. In the case of Therese and his Nanya, the other became the "counterphobic accompaniant," protective in spite of "inferiority." This inferior other gave him a sense of protection against the "wolves" of the competitive, aggressive socioeconomic world. Therese accompanied him in his efforts to confront this world—going to a university, getting a job. His Nanya was also very much in the role of the friendly, protective other.

The transference relationship was one of ambivalence and aggression against the "father," which is what Freud (1918) describes as occurring in transference with him.

THE DREAM REFRAMED

In the light of our propositions, we will reexamine the Wolf Man's most famous dream, from which he derived his name. The dream was characterized by complete motionlessness: the wolves, to whom he attributed extreme voracity and aggressiveness in his associations, were unmoving in the dream, while his fear of his own excessive rage and potential for attack was frozen and converted into a passive state in the dream.

In addition, the associations in the dream, as recorded by Freud, were those of a wolf whose tail was pulled off by the tailor when the wolf behaved aggressively. When the wolf tried to gain revenge, he was frightened off by the astute tailor. Aggression literally resulted in the wolf's losing his tail. The wolves in the other fairy stories that the Wolf Man associated with the dream were destroyed by a protective woodsman because they devoured helpless others. The avenging woodsman retaliated by killing and cutting open the wolves in the fairy tales of "Little Red Riding-Hood" and "The Wolf and the Seven Little Goats." The Wolf

Man associated Freud's grandfather clock with the need to hide from the punishment that the "woodsman"—Freud—could impose upon him if Freud found him to be "the bad wolf."

The wolves' whiteness could represent the Wolf Man's need to hide or cover up his real identity, not as the lily-white, innocent sheep, but as a voracious wolf. He referred to the wolf (Wolf Man) fooling the baker (father) by covering his paw with white flour. He also made the association that his father had not been successful in his attempt to protect the sheep. He had vaccinated them, but more had died as a result of treatment. Neither was the father effective in protecting the Wolf Man from his invading and attacking sister nor in giving him a sense of control over his destructive impulses. Therefore, the father could not be successful in helping to prepare him for a competitive life. He had been helpless in his attempts to "vaccinate" the "defenseless" Wolf Man.

As to the context of the dream, it occurred on Christmas Eve, when the Wolf Man was expecting to receive a double share of presents because it was his birthday as well. This was a time at which his voracity was at a peak. Certain feelings were probably at their maximum: that he had a right to receive and that he was treated unfairly because of his sister's superiority and consequent favored position with his father. These feelings would most likely have threatened him with the possibility that his impulsive, aggressive behavior could go out of control. In addition, the infantile neurosis occurred after an incident with the English governess. She had threatened his contact with his protective Nanya, his old, loving, but severe nurse, who had given him the sense of importance that he longed to receive from his father. This threatened change in the relationship with his Nanya was also related in time to a show of aggressive outbursts of irritability and a change in character. It marked the onset of his childhood phobias.

These hypotheses about the meaning of the dream coincide with the content of other recurring childhood dreams that are characterized by a fear of destructive, aggressive animals that could attack him. And they explain the development of his animal phobias. We find a deep unconscious bonding of fear to aggressive, assertive behavior. In fact, normal assertiveness was avoided compulsively in an attempt to avoid danger. The outcome was a perpetuation of the Wolf Man's feeling of inferiority. This, in turn, made his sister even more his father's favorite, fed his rage, and further limited his competitiveness. The scrupulous avoidance of competitive situations perpetuated his problem in that it made him continue in a weak, dependent, inferior position. The dilemma closed the circle of the repetition compulsion.

The transference relationship was to be obedient and submissive to a strong father, who must take all responsibility for a weak, dependent, and inferior Wolf Man. Great ambivalence occurred in relation to the father figure, as Freud reported. The Wolf Man also reported his excessive submissive dependence on Freud, an idealized authority, and complained that the development of transference in the therapeutic setting had tended to spread to other relations, thereby reinforcing an attitude of "trust and obey."

In his melodramatic acting out, the Wolf Man became involved with someone socially inferior and in some way economically dependent, who would tolerate his devaluations and would not abandon or destroy him. Then he could demonstrate the "inferiority" and the powerlessness of this economically dependent person. She would not be threatening to his security because of her inferior economic power. He would achieve a relative security, guaranteed company, and a false, although precarious, sense of superiority. This, at the expense of losing all possibility of achieving a state of equality and productivity. His understanding became confirmed in the acting out of his melodrama. Therefore, in his moments of greatest and most overwhelming anxiety, he reenacted the historic melodrama instead of confronting the real drama.

UNSIGNIFIED EXPERIENCE: ESSENTIAL TO SYMBOLIC TRANSFORMATION

On the deep level, the unconscious is preverbal. The important affect that organizes units of deep unconscious meaning occurred in relation to experience without any logical digital analysis of its context, other possible units of meaning, or how one experience differs from another. They were simply known as an experienced totality (Diekman 1971).

Freud (1912) proposed that reliving these memory traces through transference and putting them into words is an important part of therapy. This model would also suggest that living a consciously identified, specifically therapeutic, enriching, nonmelodramatic interpersonal experience gives a vital, new, productive, and dramatic organization to coding. This experience is necessary for the analysand to overcome compulsive melodramatic motivation. Using the therapeutic setting to carefully and specifically design experiential learning is essential to the freeing of the analysand's desire from unconscious motivation.

The Wolf Man was in accord with this position. After his many years of analysis, he offered this important comment:

> A change can occur when one experiences something that refutes what one has become used to. But memory by itself, I believe, is no use. According to Freud, remembering is enough. But I doubt that. I believe a turn can come through an experience. But it must be experienced in reality, not just in one's mind. That isn't enough. (Obholzer 1982:148)

The specific therapeutic experience for the Wolf Man would have been one in which he was accompanied and encouraged in his assertive efforts, valued realistically, rewarded for developing his own capacity. The Wolf Man would have had to be led, encouraged, pressured, or induced to act differently; otherwise he could never resolve his compulsive motivation or reorganize his motivating affects. He could have learned to feel better by acting better.

THE ACTUAL UNCONSCIOUS
AND STEREOTYPED IMAGINING

The unconscious space may be modeled in relation to *process* as well as to content. The process characteristic of this topical space is analogic: relations between symbols are the more open and less precise ones of contiguity and similarity.

In our model, the truly creative and unpredetermined analogic activity would take place in the potential unconscious because it lies outside the content constrictions of the frame. We would confine to the unconscious the primary-process activity related to the deep affect-bonded organizers and to the imagining, which is constricted by (and occurs within) the value and cognitive assumptions. Although it is analogic in its process, the creativity of the unconscious is limited to variations on a theme. That is, the unconscious is constricted to imagining possibilities consonant with existing preconscious assumptions.

Freud gives an example of this analogic, free-association type of thinking when he describes a "dumb show" put on by the Wolf Man in his office. He entered the consulting room and looked at the grandfather clock. Then he "looked at me in a very friendly way as though to propitiate me, and then turned his look away from me to the clock. . . . A long time later the patient reminded me of this piece of dumb show and gave me an explanation of it; for he recalled that the youngest of the seven little goats hid himself in the case of the grandfather clock while his six brothers were eaten by the wolf. So what he meant by this was: 'Be kind to me. Must I be frightened of you? Are you going to eat me up? Shall I hide myself from you in the clock case like the youngest little goat?' " (1918:512).

This imagining is stereotyped and is simply another variation on the persistent theme of fear of aggression. The functional similarity between his father and Freud, who acted as a father figure, created a symbolic link. The grandfather clock in Freud's office was similar to the clock found in the tale of "The Wolf and the Seven Little Goats" symbolized hiding from the danger of an attack by Father-Freud. The condensation of meaning so typical of analogic symbols was deciphered by Freud into the multiple meanings evident in the message. Although the process is analogic, the content, which comes from the unconscious, is stereotyped.

We would model other truly creative nonstereotyped imaging as taking place in the potential unconscious, beyond the constricting frame. It is capable of mutant thought, not within the valuative and cognitive assumptions or the stereotyped affect organization characteristic of the deep unconscious. Creativity can be expanded deliberately beyond constricting assumptions, as is seen in such processes as "brainstorming"; in this exercise, reality (cognitive assumptions) and morality (value assumptions) are broken by the rapid production of options when the subject has no time to judge them critically. Creative exercises also allow new articulations to be generated between events by using the openness of the analogic process to go beyond what is assumed.

6.

THE METACONSCIOUS: THE *EXTRAFRAME* ABOVE DIMENSION

The *extraframe* space is conceived as having two dimensions with distinct processes and functions. As we have said before, one space, the metaconscious, is "above" the frame because it is able to refer to the frame and to the spaces from outside of them, and another, the potential unconscious, is beyond it because it is able to enrich and expand the *intraframe* spaces and the frame itself. The metaconscious is an abstract digital dimension, capable of analyzing the preconscious frame itself as well as the logic of the *intraframe* relations. It is nondogmatic, being objectively above and outside the frame assumptions on another logical level (Popper 1972). This may be referred to as the level of tertiary thought process. Primary process is the first level of thing representation bound directly to affect. Secondary process is a digital word representation, being an elaboration of the primary thing representation. Tertiary process is thought about thought, a metarepresentation. All analytic process is digital and logical in its organization. By "digital" we mean that the representation is linguistic rather than imagistic, and the rules of analysis are logical and sequential. From this space the analysand can analyze the social and personal context of thought. He can identify the frame assumptions that delimit and organize the contents of the conscious and unconscious spaces. The Wolf Man comments, for example, on his assumption that he had been born with privileged protection and that this assumption had been invalidated dramatically when he discovered that he had gonorrhea. These comments are evaluative analytic observations on his own basic assumptions. They come from an *extraframe* analytic space able to perceive and analyze the frame. Again, when he perceived his father as not even questioning the permanence and the inevitability of this assumption, he perceived his father's socially reinforced blindness. As is always the case, he could objectively perceive and analyze the assumptions of others more readily than he could the context of his own thinking. Paradigmatic psychoanalysis contributes to the development of the analytic space as the analyst focuses on the assumptions of the analysand.

The *extraframe* metaconscious space contains nondogmatic thought, both about conscious thought and about the thinker in his social context. It is concerned with the establishment of the relatively objective point of reference, from which we study both the frame constrictions and deficits, as well as the social context in which they occur (Slawski 1974). This metaperspective questions the cognitive assumptions and analyzes the dogmatic defense. It challenges the rules of the social game and the family rules of the personal game, permitting consideration of new metarules and assumptions for totally new games.

The preconscious frame is the principal source of defense against the articulation of this *extraframe* objective information. The subject avoids the anxiety created by a challenge to his paradigm. In one mechanism to achieve impermeability, he perceives selectively what he expects to see. He dogmatically devalues dissonant material.

CONSTRUCTING AND DEVELOPING THE METACONSCIOUS

The metaconscious dimension, achieved by stepping out of the system itself and looking back at it, has been considered traditionally to provide the "analytic space" (Viderman 1970) necessary in therapy. The subject's metaconscious space may be undeveloped, in which case the therapist *educates* the analysand to think about his thoughts and about himself as an object of study. In addition, he helps him to perceive the constricting social game in the context in which he has learned to signify. The attitudes, the values, and the cultural melodramatic game are analyzed in the course of treatment. Obviously, this analysis can be undertaken because the analyst also has a well-developed metaconscious space. His own metaconscious space is one of the therapeutic tools with which he achieves the understanding of the frame.

We recount very briefly the history of Betty. She had been raised in a family in which to talk was very difficult. If her mother discovered she had been misbehaving, she was blamed and denounced to the father who would beat her. Betty did not even think much to herself. Her inner world was undeveloped. She simply acted out her wishes and then discovered their cost. Her major motivation was to "hide the facts." Her lack of symbolic elaboration made her impulsive. She acted out her sexual fantasies on various occasions until her unfaithfulness was discovered by her husband. Although he loved her and wanted to understand, she would not talk to him about what she had done, even though she knew that he had already been informed. She was absolutely convinced that no one *could* understand, anyway. When she tried to think about her unacceptable behavior, she became very anxious, dealing with herself as her mother had treated her. She assumed that the therapist, like the mother, would be punitive and accusatory. She attempted to make her sessions very chatty, without real content. One of the analytic tasks was to help her to think about and analyze her behavior.

The metaconscious space is developed with the assistance of the *extraframe* point of reference, which occurs in therapy when the analyst shows the analysand the defects in the eyes with which he sees his distorted world. The therapist brings an objective awareness of the frame assumptions, allowing the analysand to conduct a further analysis of his own suppositions once they have been made visible to him. Such an approach on the part of the parents—the identifying of values, attitudes, and assumptions, as opposed to a dogmatic attitude—is helpful in developing the metaprocess of the individual. When he has not received this early opportunity (Bion 1965), the person is likely to suffer an impermeability and closure of his *intraframe* psychic spaces, and his treatment is thus more difficult.

The metaconscious space is defined clearly here as the base from which to analyze both the thinker's context and the structuring of his thought. The analysis is conducted in a nondogmatic, objective way, or at least in a consciously identified, intersubjective or subjective way. The reason for placing this space outside the constrictions of the frame is obvious: although conscious, at the same time, being an *extraframe* nondogmatic evaluation of the frame assumptions, it is "metaconscious." For example, Betty must be able to see that others did not simply judge her. They tried to understand. How to cover up the bad was not the issue. The impulse had to be weighed against the outcome and the values she desired to pursue.

META-ANALYSIS OF FRAME LIMITS AND STRUCTURE

It is clear that we are making an important distinction between thinking about the thinker's context and thinking about thought within the frame of the preconscious assumptions, which we define as *intraframe* analytic thought and place simply on a higher level of abstraction within the *intraframe* conscious thought. This *intraframe* metalevel of thought may challenge the rules of the game, as expressed in assumed and assigned identity, but not the game itself (Lakatos and Musgrove 1968). Here the consistency, congruence, and logic of conscious thought are analyzed, but not the value and cognitive assumptions that constrict their contents. Psychoanalysis must include the metaconscious analysis of the frame as well as an analysis of *intraframe* relations.

An example of the difference between metaconscious and *intraframe* analysis is found in the reasoning of the Wolf Man's father, who wished to secure his son's future. A meta-analysis would have included an analysis of the son's possibilities for suffering some social change and of preparing him for a life in a nonprotective and competitive politicoeconomic world. We know, however, that he did not even consider these factors. He did analyze the problem within his assumptions of a continuing privileged politicoeconomic protection and decided that the protection that his son needed could be resolved on the level of tactics. His son must be protected from squandering his fortune on women. Therefore, he protected him from this possibility in his will. The Wolf Man was allowed access to his inheritance only after the age of twenty-eight. This tactic was adequate (*intraframe* analysis), but the strategy (metaconscious analysis) failed. The Wolf Man's social and personal context changed drastically in his lifetime. Foresight requires a capacity to perceive the social context and to detect evidence of imminent dramatic changes, which implies the application of a new strategy. The Wolf Man and his father were caught up in such a moment in history.

Betty also used tactics that were successful within the assumptions that the other was like her mother, moralistic, punitive, and unforgiving. She hid information and tried to protect her image. When the therapist challenged her, she became violently abusive, as her father was. It was a difficult task to get her to look at her own behavior and to analyze her strategy to hide her behavior and fool or bully others. This reevaluation could only be made if she could be brought to question her own assumptions that the other was hostile and unwilling to understand. And this was precisely the issue about which she was hostile and unwilling to understand.

Mack Brunswick (Gardiner 1971) insisted that the Wolf Man recognize his excessive dependency on Freud as pathological, and she led him to question this dependent state. What he had taken as natural and one of his rights was redefined as pathological. She attacked his frame assumptions and insisted on putting a stop to his acting out.

In summary, the metaconscious space is the analytic space from which the subject perceives his assumptions as such and is able to challenge them. Its development in treatment allows the analysand a greater flexibility and openness in his attitude and understanding.

7.
THE POTENTIAL UNCONSCIOUS: THE *EXTRAFRAME* BEYOND DIMENSION

The *extraframe* beyond dimension contains two types of representations: (1) the representations of data or information that has been registered and represented but has not yet been signified—that is, has no cognitive value or affect significance; (2) the representations of what can be experienced but has not yet been experienced, although it lies within the individual's biological and cultural limitations. Such thought is not determined by or included within the narrow organizing assumptions of the frame. It represents a dimension of nonpredetermination and creativity, which implies going beyond the mere projection of the known into the unknown. It gives the potential to what we label as the potential unconscious. Such thought occurs as a result of a creative generation of and playing with symbols, which develop in the social environment of the child (Winnicott 1971). The child may be encouraged to imagine and to seek possibilities, or his playful efforts may be disqualified dogmatically. In the latter case, the *extraframe* process is impeded in its development.

It will be seen that the analogic thought process of the potential unconscious and the objective digital process of the metaconscious are equally essential to the therapeutic process. The metaconscious space opens the system by analyzing the framing assumptions. It is thus opened to the potential unconscious, now a source of enrichment to the open system. In the case of the Wolf Man, the perception of the constrictions on his game and the incorporation of representations of cooperative, productive games would have depended on the therapeutic use of the metaconscious and potential unconscious spaces. The metaconscious would have allowed the Wolf Man to understand his basic assumption and fear about his worthlessness, while the potential unconscious would have allowed him to find a solution to his perception of himself as worthless. The Wolf Man needed his inherent worth to be reaffirmed ; he needed to be valued for himself, for his artistic contributions, or for his more mundane clerical work, and he needed to be valued in a role that contributed to relationships producing mutual benefit and happiness. He needed a specific type of new experience and needed to live this with feeling.

In the case of Peter, he must perceive and analyze the constrictions on his game of being either the suffering abandoned son or the abandoning husband or father producing suffering in those who love him. He must perceive his own tendency to overvalue an absorbing relationship, a tendency combined with his confusion of love with absolute attention. He should seek and develop relationships of the type left in his potential unconscious by the constricting paradigm. In his potential unconscious is the capacity to perceive togetherness as a symbolic state in which he and his wife are together in their project to raise a happy family, without her being absorbed in him.

In her case, Diane must perceive the constrictions on the game she plays with husband, analyst, and boyfriend, the game in which she assumes that pessimism is realism. While she tends to give up in a self-induced defeat resulting from a lack of persistence, subtle sabotaging of plans, and the undeveloped state into which she has grown as a result of many years of self defeat, in her potential unconscious is the representation of the realistic optimism she needs to experience. The representations of certain coping capacities have also remained in the potential unconscious because of her conviction that she was unable to learn.

The articulation of the contents of the potential unconscious to the frame and their inclusion in the *intraframe* spaces requires that important defenses and resistances be overcome. The information is dissonant to the assumptions and organization of the *intraframe* spaces (Brehm and Cohen 1966). It is not repressed, as is information in the unconscious, in the deep unconscious material. A characteristic feature of this information is its meaninglessness because it lies outside the cognitive and valuative assumptions. It is also nonmotivating since it has no established positive affect significance. The potential unconscious space contains the qualitatively new experience necessary for the therapeutic tasks of freeing, enriching, and fulfilling desire.

In Betty's case, it contains the relationship of knowing and understanding as opposed to the *intraframe* relationship of detecting and denouncing or angrily attacking one who denounces. Betty had a difficult time registering the nonjudgmental attitude of the therapist to whom she attributed the role of a moral judge who must be fooled.

REPRESENTING WITHOUT SIGNIFYING

It is not uncommon for an individual to register experience to which he can give no meaning. Freud shows his awareness of this phenomenon in his argument in favor of a "primal scene." He suggests that the Wolf Man experienced a primal scene when he was one and one-half years old. Freud, however, believed that the experience remained without significance until the Wolf Man reached the age of four, when he was able to give it meaning and to react to it affectively. People do tend to recall experiences that cannot be given meaning—when a gestalt cannot be closed. New knowledge suddenly makes them comprehensible. The reader can recall events in his childhood that he could not understand but did not forget and that were given meaning later in his life.

Information may be given meaning in a distorted way. The Wolf Man's concept of what it is to be ill psychologically, for example, seems to have excluded the possibility of recognizing signs of mental illness in his wife. Obholzer finds it hard to believe that the Wolf Man did not know from her behavior that Therese was depressed. She inquired of him: "Your wife found it difficult to establish contact, she wanted to go nowhere and isolated herself more and more. Isn't that a sign that there is something wrong?" The Wolf Man replied: "I noticed nothing. Weakness of the will didn't exist for her. She had no need for authority" (1982:103).

Outside the limits of understanding, in the potential unconscious, was the understanding that firmness of will was not equivalent to mental health. The Wolf Man's wife was sure in her opinions and therefore healthy. He read the signs from his own cognitive set. For him, mental health would have been assertiveness and strength of will.

GAMES AND THE POTENTIAL UNCONSCIOUS SPACE

We will examine the information essential to health but left in the potential unconscious first, on the level of the social convictions and context— the social game and the family version of the social game; second, on the level of the politicoeconomic paradigm of understanding—the dependency-control game; and third, on the level of the interpersonal paradigm —the sadomasochistic melodramatic game.

1. The Social Game

On the level of the social context and the social game, it is important to determine the game that is present in an obvious way and the game that, although essential to the fulfillment of the individual's conscious desire, is absent from his *intraframe* spaces. Social assumptions exclude certain perceptions and actions from the problem solving space.

For example, the Wolf Man was unable to perceive the outcome of his immediate social context. He left Russia only four months before the Revolution without realizing that he must protect his fortune. An appreciation of the imminent danger did not intrude upon his awareness until shortly after he resumed his treatment with Freud. He described the social convictions of those times as follows:

> Well, those were completely different times. People believed in progress and thought that the condition of mankind could only improve. That things couldn't get worse. About Russia, people believed that if democracy came it would be paradise. (Obholzer 1982:38)

In the context of such optimism, there was nothing to fear and no need to concern oneself with saving the fortune. We could say that the representation of the information about imminent catastrophe was not a part of the constricted system because it was dissonant to the socially shared representation of change as equivalent to improvement. The error was also reinforced by the father's conviction that the condition of privilege and entitlement would continue unchanged and that the son's only danger was the possibility of squandering the family fortune on women of ill repute.

The immediate social context of Vienna further reinforced the Wolf Man's sense of social stability, reaffirming that the social game of entitlement and aristocratic privilege would continue, as the Wolf Man says:

> Vienna was completely different, the capital of an empire, with lots of soldiers. That gave the city a certain splendor. . . . It was magnificent, how interesting, how witty, how intelligent. (39)

This atmosphere certainly favored the Wolf Man's desire for diversion and for splendor and probably reduced the alarm that he might have felt at this grave potential threat to his politicoeconomic security (Backman, Secord, and Pierce 1963). The assumption that change could be regressive rather than inevitably beneficial for him (Clausen 1968) would not have occurred to him in such a context.

The forced alteration in the social game—the loss of his fortune and the forced immigration to Austria, with the need to work as a bureaucratic clerk in an insurance company—must have been a major source of stress in the Wolf Man's life. Freud refers only vaguely to this change because his interest in reporting the case was to demonstrate the infantile neurosis. In addition, the treatment began before this social upheaval. Our own clinical experience and theoretical position give great importance to such environmental events and to the process of incorporating them into understanding.

We believe that the Wolf Man should have taken the social context into account and have dealt directly with the dramatic changes in order for his therapy to have been successful. Of course, he would not have understood nor have had the skills for a social game without special entitlement and aristocratic privilege. Therefore, he would have attempted to compensate by creating a confirming environment in which his value assumptions could have continued to be shared. He would probably have tried to avoid confrontation with the difficult task of making the necessary changes in his relation to the socioeconomic world and would have continued the game of privilege.

Indeed, this is what the Wolf Man did. He continued to seek to be indulged, spoiled, and protected—even by Freud. One of Mack Brunswick's major efforts (Gardiner 1971) was directed at forcing him to become more independent, to take into account the new social context, and to articulate this information to the existing social and family assumptions.

The Wolf Man did not know that a social game directed at real productivity even existed. His game was focused on the unfair distribution of the benefits and pleasures already available. Even worse, for him the problem was how to distribute displeasure unfairly; the issue was one of entitlement, not productivity. In the Wolf Man's aristocratic, reactionary paradigm and in the complementary proletarian, revolutionary paradigm, major concern was with the distribution of what already existed. A paradigm not based on privilege was not meaningful (Adams 1965). For the Wolf Man, the aristocratic family game of superiority-inferiority and of excessive entitlement was meaningful in that social context. However, the games based on equity theory and the importance of increased productivity (Cook 1975) were actively excluded, being repudiated and remaining in the potential unconscious.

2. The Politicoeconomic Game

For the Wolf Man, the socioeconomic was totally subordinated to the interpersonal. On the level of socioeconomic understanding, the Wolf Man used his economic resources to play the melodramatic interpersonal game. He did not conceive of the value of socioeconomic achievement in itself. In the interviews with Obholzer (1982), it was she who commented on the pleasure of having published a book (his autobiography), stating: "And that does something for you. That a book you wrote was published." He replied: "Well, that's vanity" (108).

To the Wolf Man it did not seem vain to take clothing excessively into account, to need to be admired personally for his economic power, or to need to be superior to the women in his life. It seemed unacceptable, however, to take pride and joy from the completion of a productive effort.

He consistently used his economic and social power to structure his melodrama, in which he could devalue a partner—usually a woman—and insist she accept this devaluation because of economic dependence. Examples of this abuse of economic power are innumerable. He spoke in these terms of Therese, Luise, and countless servant women.

A vital absence in what is signified in the constricted spaces is the use of socioeconomic power to fulfill desire and to solve dramatic problems. For a healthy person, power is used to produce happiness rather than to assure the unjust distribution of displeasure. For the Wolf Man, this information had not been signified but remained in the potential unconscious.

3. The Interpersonal Game

On the level of the interpersonal paradigm, there was no reference in the Wolf Man's speech to mutually respectful and valuing relations between people. The constrictions of his frame made him aware only of the relations of exploitation, victimization, and inferiority. On innumerable occasions he referred to the social status of the other but not to the other's productivity. He usually saw the purpose of relationships as that of exploiting others economically. He polarized these relationships: people were either abusive and dominant or abused and submissive.

Within the assumed and assigned roles of the melodramatic game, there is a bipolar splitting (Klein 1975) in the representation of categories of human roles in the melodrama. For the Wolf Man the roles were those of the "exploiter-exploited" or the "superior-inferior." The option of equality and mutual benefit was not represented, or, if it was, it was not motivating or truly meaningful within the Wolf Man's value constrictions. These categories were absent, and could be said to have existed only in his potential unconscious. In such cases, they must be introduced into the system in the process of therapy (Gear, Liendo, and Scott 1983).

OPERATIONAL DEFICITS

The Wolf Man lacked certain interpersonal skills necessary to fulfill the desire for happiness, especially in relation to the interpersonal code after the Russian Revolution. He was quite capable of exploiting, dominating, and mistreating people, such as Therese and the Russian servants, who were accustomed to accept their roles. However, with a psychopathic woman like Luise, he was totally unable to hold his own. His gentlemanly ways and rather silly tricks to avoid involvement were absolutely ineffective. Obviously, he was deficient in the development of the skills necessary to dominate and exploit someone such as Luise. His skills were more appropriate to exploiting those with a feudal set of assumptions.

Fortunately, in the socioeconomic area, Therese had supported the Wolf Man in his plan to go to the university. Again, he attributed to her presence the fact that he could somehow find a way to stay on as an insurance clerk, in spite of the boring routine. The skills necessary for effective socioeconomic problem-solving and planning were outside his learning experience. He simply had *not* been prepared. To have found happiness he must somehow have developed a minimal amount of new social and economic skills. (The Wolf Man's specific problem-solving deficits will be further elaborated in Part II.)

ARTICULATING THE VALUATIVELY DISSONANT

The introduction of valuatively dissonant material is much more difficult than the simple introduction of the unknown that is nevertheless consonant with the frame assumptions. It would have been easier to teach the Wolf Man a new language than to have changed his idea that Therese was inferior because she did not speak French. The new language, although not yet known, is not dissonant to the system as the system stands, whereas the latter information is dissonant and requires an accomodation of the system itself (Asch 1952). This type of material is repudiated by the value and cognitive structure of the system. It presses to enter because the solution to real problems is dependent on its being included. Its exclusion results in a return of the repudiated since the problem is not solved and the failure recurs.

That which is *extraframe* and dissonant is actively selected out. It is not motivating; it is valuatively denigrated; and it is incompatible with the cognitive assumptions.

The aspect of nonpredetermination in the potential unconscious exists because the potential unconscious lies beyond the constrictions of the already known. It is not, however, totally unconditioned; biological and cultural limitations always condition the thinkability of any thought.

The creative imagining of the primal scene, for example, went beyond the assumptions of Freud's times and of his own prior theorizing. Yet his creative thought was conditioned by the theoretical propositions of Jung (1977) and Adler (1955), by the models used in biology and physics at that time, and by Freud's own exceptional biological potential for creative imagination.

THERAPEUTIC RELEVANCE OF THE
POTENTIAL UNCONSCIOUS

The function of the therapist does not stop at opening a relatively objective metaconscious dimension. It also includes the incorporation of information from the dissonant beyond dimension of the potential unconscious, giving a new frame that is significantly expanded in relation to its original narrow dimensions. The expansion and enrichment contribute to the reorganization of desire and make new projects for happiness imaginable. Each topical dimension has a distinct importance in the therapeutic process.

The need for the creation of this expanded topological model responds finally to an important clinical deficit. It has been assumed that psychoanalysis could limit itself to dealing with the content of the unconscious — that is, what was already present was what was important. Our clinical experience made it clear to us that what was not included into the *intraframe* symbol system was often essential to the subject's dealing with current problems. The deficits on the symbolic level must be treated as well as the defenses and resistances.

Again, we are impressed clinically by the importance of frame impermeability and rigidity in the psychic system, which impedes the introduction of new essential and enriching information. To open the space requires that the frame be perceived and analyzed from a point of reference outside the constricting assumptions of the system itself. How to reframe the frame and how to increase the openness of the system to a new potential become new dimensions for therapy. These will be dealt with in Part III.

II

DESIRE AND ITS FULFILLMENT

8.

DUAL CODING IN ITS
HISTORICAL PERSPECTIVE

The dual coding modes that we identify as analogic thing representation, characteristic of the right hemisphere, and digital word representation, characteristic of the left hemisphere, will be examined here in their distinct but complementary coding functions (Nebes 1974), both on the level of structuring desire and on the level of the fulfilling of conscious desire. A reexamination of Freud's modeling of the dual codes, which he represented in primary and secondary process, will be undertaken and compared to recent experimental findings. The implications of this recent experimental and theoretical knowledge about dual coding will be explored and integrated into dynamic theory. We will examine the two coding modes in terms of the nature of their symbols, purposes, processes, principles of functioning and forms of organization and reorganization and in terms of their implications in health and pathology. This reformulation has important therapeutic implications on two levels. First, on the level of affect and motivation, the analogic code has been found to be organized primarily by affect; the digital code is organized primarily by logic and related only secondarily to affect in a way derived from the logical organization (Zajonc 1980). We will propose this difference as determining the very important discrepancy that exists in mental illness between the two motivating forces—conscious and unconscious desire. Therefore, we can readdress such important mental health questions as these: Why does a person continue to do what has become self-defeating in terms of his conscious purpose and his current potential? Is man irrational or arational in certain important behaviors? What can be done to modify unconscious desire and to free the subject from his compulsion to repeat the only game playable by him in the interpersonal context of his infancy? How is the affect organization of the analogic system changed?

Second, on the level of fulfilling what is consciously desired, the digital and the analogic coding functions are taken to be equally essential in the analysand's problem-solving efforts as he struggles to fulfill his conscious desire (Aylesworth and Reagan 1966). The analogic primary code is essential for generating options, for creative efforts, for holistic or heuristic understanding, and for imagining new potential, while the digital is equally essential for logical deductive and factorial analysis and for the organizing and sequencing of operational plans and procedures (Newell and Simon 1972).

Coding deficits in the analogic or digital mode or in the level of abstraction and degree of integration developed in each mode will be proposed as determinants of general learning and thinking styles. These styles have their own strengths and deficits (Harrison and Bronson 1983). The deficits are found to produce characteristic difficulties in problem-solving behavior and therefore impede the fulfillment of desire, while the strengths are useful in the special skills that the person brings to his potential for the fulfillment of desire. The therapeutic strategy will include playing into strengths and correcting or consciously compensating for weaknesses.

Thus, the dual coding model allows us to take yet another angle in viewing deficits in coding and problem-solving behavior, as well as correcting these deficits in the therapeutic process. Health will be related to the balanced (whole-brain) development of the two codes and to the degree to which they are applied appropriately (Kolb 1984).

FREUD'S DUAL CODING MODEL: A REVIEW

The existence of two distinct coding modes, called primary and secondary process, was first formulated by Freud in "The Project for a Scientific Psychology" (1895). "Primary" was used in a double sense: as "primitive" and as "prior"—prior in that it was the thing representation; secondary was subsequent because it was the word representation of this thing representation. In addition, primary was historically the earlier and more primitive form of coding, being the preverbal code used by the newborn infant, whereas secondary coding was historically later and required the development of language.

In addition to nourishing his interest in the two types of *symbols,* Freud's discovery of the unconscious (1915b) and his work on dreams gave him a base on which to model unconscious primary thought as a *symbol system,* to describe its significant differences from conscious secondary process, and to establish the "rules" of translation from one mode to another (1900). Freud then linked the two codes to his topical, economic, and dynamic model of the psychic apparatus. Of course, he also defined the characteristics of each thought mode and the relation between them and psychopathology.

Topical Relations

Topically, according to Freud (1915b), primary process characterizes the unconscious system, while secondary process characterizes the preconscious-conscious system. He recognized later that the unconscious also contained repressed verbal material. That is, the unconscious was characterized as containing defensively repressed material and was not confined to one coding mode, although the process characteristic of the unconscious was primary.

Economic Relations

Freud linked primary and secondary process to psychic energy in two distinct ways. In the case of primary process, he described psychic energy as flowing freely, passing without impediment from one representation to another by way of the mechanisms of displacement and condensation. It tends to charge fully the representations linked to the experience of satisfaction making up desire (wish cathexis). This modeling corresponds to more recent evidence that the analogic, right-hemisphere code organizes and understands experience in terms of affect categories. Its decision process is emotional. The decisions are based on "preferenda," what is emotionally preferred in accord with the affect significance given to the experience (Zajonc 1980). In addition, the analogic thing representations, as symbols, are themselves more imprecise and polysemic. The relations that link the different symbols are those of contiguity and similarity, not logic.

In the case of secondary process, according to Freud, the representations are charged in a more stable way: satisfaction is delayed, thus permitting mental experience that allows a trial of different ways in which satisfaction is possible (ego cathexis and reality principle). Conditions exist for distinguishing a perception of reality from a memory image. In identity of thought, characteristic of secondary process, the criteria are logical discrimination, reason, and judgment, not simply the intensity of affect in relation to a primitive wish. This process corresponds to the digital, left-hemispheric, logically organized code, which makes decisions on the basis of "discriminata" (Zajonc 1980), relating symbols in a logical way and using an analysis of the relation of thought to real possibilities. This process, of course, functions under the reality principle.

Dynamic Relations

Dynamically, the primary process, which is wish-cathected, is responsible for the conflict between unconscious and conscious desire (wish cathexis and ego cathexis). Again, according to Freud's model, the cathected ego functions to inhibit the primary-process invasion of reality functions. In health, that is, secondary process *controls* primary process. The structuring of this model assumes opposition between primary- and secondary-process functions. Freud's model, then, strongly associates primary process with pathology, whereas more recent advances in dual coding theory emphasize the general complementarity of the dual codes in their distinct functions.

Primary Process as Pathological: A Frame Constriction

Freud was not only a pioneer who went beyond what was known, but an observing clinician. We must assume that his interest in symptom formation and dreams, as well as his observations of compulsive behavior that was motivated by forces not within the reality principle, focused his interest on the relationship between the process that he identified as primary and its relation to psychopathology.

As a result, the frame of Freud's theory tends to limit primary process to sickness and primitiveness, while linking secondary process to healthy complexity and to the ego functions necessary for realistic action. This assumption results in an important misunderstanding of the relationship between analogic coding and health. Nondefensive and nonpathological thinking, such as sudden insights, holistic intuitive comprehensions, and creative breakthroughs—all of which strongly characterized Freud's own thinking and therapeutic technique—are a part of healthy analogic thought. An understanding of the two processes as complementary rather than competitive allows a new understanding of the importance of the analogic code to health.

Characteristics of the Dual Modes

Here we summarize our understanding of the distinctions and characteristics of these two processes, as given by Freud.

Primary	Secondary
Thing representation	Word representation
Condensation	Stable discriminating representation
Displacement	
Overdetermination	
Wish	Desire
Wish cathexis	Ego cathexis
Hallucinated gratification	Real gratification
Pleasure principle	Reality principle
Immediate discharge	Planned action

9.

DUAL CODING RECONSIDERED

More impressive than any shortcomings in Freud's model is the fact that he could make such a clear clinical identification of two types of thought processes, with dual coding systems involving distinct symbols, mechanisms, and principles of operation. The questions he attempted to answer —the relation of coding to affect (Laplanche and Leclaire 1961), the problem of unconscious motivation and the repetition compulsion, the relation of the codes to health and pathology—remain central to more modern theories. The answers Freud gave intuitively went far beyond the conceptual constrictions of his times, representing what we would call a breakthrough beyond the actually known or logically deducible into the creative potential of his own potential unconscious. At that time, he could not formalize these breakthroughs with the precision possible today, when we have the privilege of looking at his insights from the perspective of a much more highly developed body of scientific information on coding.

Because of recent advances in cognitive theory, we can reconsider dual coding in terms of topical relations; the complexity of analogic thought; the anatomical location of the two symbol systems; the relationship between the functions of the analogic and the digital codes in health and pathology; the development of a coding and learning style; and the relationship of the affect organization of the primary code to compulsive unconscious motivation.

90

THE EXPANDED TOPOLOGY AND THE DUAL CODE

In our topological model, we define the contents of the superficial unconscious in the dynamic sense of repressed content, not process, and include the defensively coded content of both the analogic and the digital modes. Digital thought at any stage of development can be repressed into the superficial unconscious as a result of its value or its cognitive unacceptability.

The deep unconscious is totally analogic; the early experience is coded in the analogic primary mode. Not only are the symbols preverbal, but, more importantly, the organization has a distinct form, in which the corporal affect and the experience are bonded in an inseparable unit, which gives the timeless organization to the contents of the deep unconscious. The relations established to affect are not subject to logic, and this primary material is very difficult to change. The analogic affect code is the source of the unconscious compulsive motivation to reproduce experience with a certain affect meaning and to avoid other experience that has a traumatic affect significance (Gear and Liendo 1976).

The modeling of the constricted conscious and the preconscious spaces includes both analogic and digital double coding. In consciousness, analogic thought is characterized by thinking in analogy, metaphor, and example and by the visualizing of complex patterns (Edwards 1979). The digital code is used in conscious logical deductive thinking (Berliner 1977). In the preconscious frame, the analogic code is used to represent the informal assumptions and paradigm of understanding, while the digital code represents the formal logical hypotheses and formal theories derived from the informal paradigms. Therefore, a dual representation exists in the constricting preconscious, the constricted conscious, and the superficial unconscious. The dual codes simultaneously fulfill complementary roles, both of which are necessary in healthy problem-solving and motivating functions (Gear and Liendo 1979).

In the *extraframe* analytic metaconscious and creative potential unconscious dimensions of the expanded topology described in Part I, the metaconscious space is modeled as the logical, analytic, digital dimension. It is concerned with the logical evaluation and analysis of the structure of the preconscious frame, as well as its dogmatic valuative defense and its unquestioned cognitive assumptions. It represents the highest level of development of the digital code. Being on distinct metalevel, it could be considered a tertiary process—as thought about secondary process thought. The potential unconscious is analogic, and it is responsible for creative free associations, possibility generation, and other such processes. It represents the broadest level of development of the analogic code. Like Winnicott (1971), we place the process that is neither compulsively organized nor defensively repressed—that which represents creative associative thinking—in the potential unconscious. In addition, we place in the potential unconscious the thing representations that have been symbolized but not signified and the representations of what can be experienced but has not yet been experienced. That is, the potential unconscious is modeled in terms of both process and content. Integration of information from it depends upon the digital metaconscious analysis of the frame constrictions. Again, the digital and the analogic functions are equally essential and complementary in health.

ANALOGIC COMPLEXITY IN SYMBOLS AND PROCESS

Although imagery may be defined as an isomorphic analogue to perception, the analogic process does not limit itself to this concrete level. It has a *conceptual* as well as a perceptual component. Although tied to the concrete in being an isomorph as a representational symbol, this process is also capable of going beyond the specificity of immediate experience. It represents a mode of thought that establishes a different kind of relationship to the mode that characterizes logico-deductive linear and digital thinking (Kagen and Kogan 1970).

The analogic system is best conceived as having distinct rather than more primitive functions. These functions seem to emphasize integration, pattern detection, and affect commitment. At the age of only a few weeks, in fact, the infant has been found to integrate information from distinct sensory modes without prior learning experience (Cooper 1983). The same infant can be shown to organize experience into affect-determined categories and to classify by developing complex prototypes. When the infant is exposed to a variety of human faces, for instance, he creates a class that could be considered to represent the mathematical average of these faces. The child prefers this composite representation or prototype, which is a complex relational construct achieved without the use of words or logic. It would appear, therefore, that complex and prewired categorizing, organizing, and integrating functions exist in the right hemisphere, just as complex and prewired analytic, and logical functions exist in left-hemispheric thinking. Both systems are equally capable of complexity, albeit of different types.

DISTINCT LOCATIONS, DISTINCT FUNCTIONS

In their work with patients who had undergone surgical division of the two hemispheres, Sperry, Gazzaniga, and Bogen (1969) were able to assign an anatomical location to these two thinking processes. They demonstrated that the digital functions of the left hemisphere are responsible for verbal and logical thinking, whereas the right hemisphere is primarily responsible for complex analogic functions such as pattern detection and temporospatial integrations. It can be said that Sperry, Gazzaniga, and Bogen (1969) broke the "silence" of the right hemisphere. Subjects with surgically split brains could be shown to have registered information introduced to the right side of the brain, although they could not express a conscious awareness of its presence. Their behavioral responses showed that they understood the information, just as information can be shown to be understood in the preverbal infant. In commissurotomized subjects, exposing the left brain to stimuli resulted in a state of what we recognize as conscious and verbalized knowing, whereas exposure of the right hemisphere resulted in an unconscious knowing, demonstrable in the subject's actions and emotional reactions. This difference in awareness was not related to the repression of the unacceptable; it was related to the silence but not the unknowingness of the wordless right brain.

Other researchers have identified the hypothalamic limbic areas as the source of the affect charge, which organizes the meaning in right-hemispheric analogic code. The left-brain code, being organized by logic, seems to have a secondary relation to affect. In the analogic code, the affect organizes the code, whereas in the digital code, logic organizes the code and affect is related only secondarily. The neurophysiological concepts are offered as a possible explanation for the psychiatric patient who manifests alexithymia (Ten Houten et al. 1985). That is, an excessive domination of left-hemispheric style is related to the concrete, unimaginative, unemotional alexithymic style.

It would appear that individuals code dually and use the analogic code in all stages of life, not only in the preverbal phase or in pathological states. The two codes are best conceived as always present, but used for distinct and complementary functions. The analogic code is a desire-structuring, possibility-generating, creative code, whereas the digital code is a reality-testing code dedicated to making dreams come true. One code imagines new possibilities and new options; the other tests plans and orders actions to achieve the imagined possibilities. The therapist's role is to help the subject to develop a whole-brain understanding and to use these distinct processes appropriately.

The previously mentioned case of Betty shows an example of someone whose coding function was incomplete. She developed her analogic functions while avoiding the precision and enclosure that would have allowed her "mother-husband-analyst" to know what she was doing and to punish her for it. Her analogic style was associated with learning by doing and by experience. She was impulsive and had been unfaithful. Her impulsiveness also brought her difficulties with other women in the community. She did not measure their envy or their resentment in relation to her actions. Her disciplining of the children had more to do with her mood than with their behavior. Betty was a poor strategist, thinking very little about her own future. She did what her emotions commanded and her decisions lacked reality testing. They were not reviewed by her own logico-digital secondary process.

In one session, Betty entered obviously angry. She lay on the couch for twenty minutes without saying a word. When asked what was wrong, she told the analyst to keep quiet since he wouldn't understand anyway. Her transference relationship with the therapist was to project onto him the attitudes of her mother and then to treat him with a verbal violence stemming from her hostility at the imagined lack of comprehension. Her usually chatty, evasive style was replaced by open hostility. At the close of the session, she broke the silence to recount a vision, or waking dream, that she had experienced during the hour. She saw her son standing in mud up to his knees, holding eight flags, and looking very sad and alone. She tried to help him but was unable to understand. The analyst interpreted the vision that she was the child, sad and alone and incomprehensible in her messages, even to herself. It was impossible to give meaning to the eight flags at the time, but in a later session, it became apparent through her free associations that the eight flags represented the eight months of treatment and the many messages incomprehensible to herself that she had tried to understand. She confessed a rage with the analyst on the day of this daydream because she had perceived him as not understanding as a result of a remark made by her husband that neither he nor anyone else could possibly understand her behavior. She did not elaborate her doubts; she attacked as her father had done, arbitrarily and without understanding. The analogic process was isolated from secondary process elaboration. Her imagining was the stereotyped imagining of her constricted intraframe symbolic world.

MECHANISMS OF CONDENSATION AND DISPLACEMENT

If we look at the nature of analogic and digital symbols and the organization of the dual symbol systems, we can contribute to the explanation behind Freud's clinical observation that condensation and displacement are mechanisms of primary process.

Condensation would be seen in dual coding theory as typical of the analogic symbols themselves (Jung 1964). The analogic symbol includes and represents many possibilities without stating clearly which of the potential meanings or which aspect of the symbol is to be accepted as significant in these circumstances. That is, as a result of the vagueness of the representation, the symbol is inclusive and polysemic, whereas the digital code is more precise and exclusive, thus condensing meaning in the symbol to a lesser degree and being less polysemic. In Freud's analysis of the Wolf Man's transmission of multiple messages in his "dumb show" with the grandfather clock, we see how the analogic symbol included many meanings in one representation. The Wolf Man simply looked at the grandfather clock and then at Freud in a pleading way. For the Wolf Man, the clock recalled the scene of the seven little goats, the youngest of which had hidden in the grandfather clock to save himself from the wolf. Once Freud was told the associations, he was able to derive the condensed meaning. He translated the action as meaning "Be kind to me. Are you going to eat me up? Must I be frightened of you? Shall I hide myself from you?" (1918:512).

Again, the analogic symbol of the wolf image represents a thousand

words. It means at the same time voracious, predator, aggressively destructive, destroyed by his aggressions, endangered, and dangerous. The
inclusiveness of the symbol results in a condensation of meaning.

The links among symbols are also more networking and generalizing,
and the Wolf Man's fear of wolves can be seen in this way. The wolf
symbol was present in many of the fairy stories of his childhood; the wolf
was an aggressor who was finally destroyed by a more powerful other—
the woodsman. Although we believe that the Wolf Man's underlying fear
was of his own aggression and retaliation by the father, this fear had been
partially displaced or generalized more broadly in his representational
system so that it could be provoked by a storybook picture, with which
his sister used to frighten him. This phobia was coincidental in time and
the "woodsman-wolf" relationship was similar in kind to that of the
"father-son." The woodsman, an aggressor himself, in danger from a
more powerful force, was categorized affectively in the class of "endan-
gered-dangerous" and could evoke the unit of feeling-experience the Wolf
Man found most traumatic, that of the fear of voracious aggression. The
picture of the wolf became "the same as" voracious aggression, and he
avoided the picture and reacted to it as if it were the threat. In later years,
a professor with the name of "Wolf"—linking similarity of name and
function (an authority figure)—provoked the same traumatic emotion.
The professor evoked the same reaction as the thought of the Wolf Man's
relationship with his father would have evoked. Thus, displacement is
linked to the thought form. Emphasis on similarity, on multiple meaning
of images, and on relatedness by contiguity contribute to the mechanisms
of displacement and overdetermination, which characterize the analogic
code.

We have had occasion to experience the mechanism of analogic coding
with condensation, displacement, and a strongly and directly linked charge
of negative affect in an adolescent who consulted two years after a gang
rape. The patient would visualize the faces of her aggressors and experienced great panic when out alone on the street at night. She felt that she
was reliving the experience each time she was in circumstances similar to
those related to the attack. With time, the stimulus that provoked the
attack of fear became more generalized. Going to the movies alone, going
to a party, going for a walk on a crowded street became triggers for the
emotional response. The patient had never elaborated the experience. She
had not told her parents for fear of reprisals and for the great unpleasant-

ness that thinking about what had occurred produced in her. The symbols had remained analogic and were bonded to an overwhelming affect charge.

This organization of the analogic system, by contiguity and similarity rather than by logic, permits the divergent networking relations among symbols that are responsible in health for the creative, imaginative, non-deducible, synthetic, and inductive aspects of problem-solving, such as generation of options and pattern detection (Torrence 1984). In illness, the imagining remains stereotyped and isolated from reality relations.

DIGITAL AND ANALOGIC COMPLEMENTARITY

The functions of the analogic and digital systems are complementary. Failure in problem-solving can be related to an excessive, unbalanced, or inappropriate use of one psychic mode—digital or analogic. The imaginative, possibility-generating mode that should be used to generate options may be used, for example, to determine action without realistic evaluation of costs and consequences. Betty is a good example. In other cases, the subject may continue to generate options and never proceed to develop concrete plans of action. He is fascinated with the possibilities that he generates but does not take advantage of them in terms of developing plans for their use in conducting his life. The analogic system is not pathological; reality testing is simply not its function. Rather, it has motivating and possibility-generating functions. It could be equated more properly to the "possibility principle."

In health, the possibilities generated analogically are evaluated by the use of secondary-process functions before action is undertaken. The relationship of these two processes is complementary. When this secondary elaboration fails to take place primary process is, of course, used inappropriately, and the subject shows a pathological impulsiveness and disregard for the conditions of reality. In Freud's terms, "primary process has invaded ego functions." What is pathological is the misuse of the analogic system, not the system itself.

Bion (1967) anticipated this emphasis on the healthy functions of the analogic system. Neri (1982), in his conception of microhallucinations in the process of therapeutic enrichment, also emphasized the healthy potential of analogic symbolization.

CHARACTERISTICS OF THE DUAL CODE

The following list includes some of the most important distinguishing characteristics of the dual codes as conceived today:

Digital	Analogic
Word	Thing
Components	Totalities
Analysis	Synthesis
Distinction	Similarity
Convergent	Divergent
Linear hierarchy	Network
Unit	Pattern
Logic	Intuition
Affect-linked	Affect-organized
Formal abstract relations	Temporospatial contiguity
Goals	Possibilities
Meta	Mega

CODING FUNCTIONS IN HEALTH AND PATHOLOGY

The dual coding system functions according to principles that are commensurate with the objectives and specialized functions of the two systems. One of the two principal functions of the analogic code is the generation of new possibilities. In health, therefore, this code is responsible for the changeable thought characteristic of the potential unconscious, with which the subject generates new questions and solves new problems as significant changes in circumstances make old solutions inoperative or inefficient. The other function of the analogic system is the structuring of desire and motivation by coding the deep unconscious affect-experience bonded unit on which desire depends. Even in healthy subjects, the bonding of the affect-experience unit makes modification of desire difficult when social—and especially interpersonal—reality changes. Motivation does not change readily in accord with the new potential for the development of new desires; that is, the sadomasochistic desire persists on the unconscious level, even when the conscious desire of secondary process has changed. This phenomenon is related to the subject's avoidance of the major affect cost of symbolic change (Walker and Heyns 1967).

Avoiding the price results in a motivation to compulsion toward the historically desired, as represented in the subject's repetition compulsion. In pathology, therefore, there is an overdetermination of outcome, the opposite of free development of possibilities. The end result is invariable in spite of changes in circumstances and variations in the starting point of transactions, in relation to strongly affect-charged material. Therefore, in health, the analogic system obeys the possibility principle and is in touch with the *extraframe* potential unconscious, whereas in sickness, especially as manifested in the irrelevant and melodramatic sadomasochistic inter-personal games, it obeys the "compulsion principle."

In relation to this bonded unit, there is not only an overdetermination of desire but also a corresponding overdetermination of associative links. Freud described this pathological aspect of the analogical as obeying the pleasure principle and linked it to cathected wish. We consider it not so much wished for; it is probably more closely related to that which is feared, which the subject tries to avoid. It always, however, represents a compulsion—an overdetermination. The unconscious analogic affect bonding is responsible for the associative chains—the locked associations so often referred to as free associations. Betty always imagined that the other could not understand her. Her free association in her daydream was of her son not being understood. Her resentment was toward the thera-pist whom she imagined as not understanding.

The stereotyped nature of the imaginings of the psychotic are known to all. The paranoid may imagine persecution by the policeman in the city or by some wild animal in the jungle, but he always imagines a relation-ship of pursuit. We are reminded of the winner of a competition for the greatest degree of imagination when he replied to the stimulus of a white handkerchief that he imagined sex. When the judges, impressed by this leap of imagination, asked him what in a white handkerchief made him think of sex, he replied that he always thought of sex.

The healthy analogic system cannot be expected to obey the reality principle because the system is not concerned with reality testing but simply with imaginable possibilities and with the structuring of desire and motivation. Wishing is a first step in the process of making things so. Generated possibilities must then be submitted to tests of reality before they are acted upon. This testing involves a complementary digital elabo-ration and is a function of the digital coding system.

The healthy digital system has the function of testing reality: that is, calculating probabilities, risk and gain, and making realistic decisions for

action. It also functions on the level of the metaspace to give objectivity
—that is, to perceive the subject and his frame constrictions. It functions
on the *intraframe* metalevel when examining the logical inner congruence
of the system of understanding. In pathology, the dogmatic principle
qualifies the frame constrictions valuatively as good or as what ought to
be and rationalizes real outcomes or incongruences rather than perceiving
them rationally.

10.

CODING STYLE

In any subject's representation of reality and thinking processes, both the analogic and the digital modes are used on varying levels of abstraction, either simultaneously or alternately, in what Freud called "thing representation" and "word representation" and in what are now commonly called the "right" and "left hemispheric" modes. Following Freud's emphasis on the type of symbol, we refer to these as "analogic" (thing) and "digital" (word) modes. We propose that although all subjects code dually, it is demonstrable that they have consistent preferences, strengths, and weaknesses (specific deficits), which are reflected in their thinking and learning styles (Jung 1964; Messick 1976; Harrison and Bronson 1983; Kolb 1984). Some subjects are more strongly emotional and analogic and tend to learn by experiencing; others are more strongly digital and logical and tend to learn verbally.

We suggest that the coding, thinking, and learning style characteristic of the analysand predisposes him to the strengths and deficits that he shows in his conceptual, strategic, and operational problem-solving procedures (Singler, Wilensky, and Craven 1956).

Fortunately, in the formation of couple relationships, opposites seem to attract. One member compensates the other in the symbolic strengths and weakness characteristic of each.

Betty, with her analogic style, was married to George, a very strongly digital thinker. He was unable even to imagine the illogical. For him, issues were black and white. His wife either loved him or she did not. The idea of someone holding two conflicting positions was simply impossible for him to conceptualize. He always demanded a logical explanation and was not at peace until he received it. When his daughter unthinkingly jumped off a swing and hurt herself, he was very disturbed and could not accept that her reason was that she wanted to see what it was like to fly through the air. His decisions were made after an extensive analysis and were not emotionally determined. His talk was matter of fact, without metaphor or the discussion of dreams in his sessions. He wanted the truth and preferred to receive concrete instructions about what to do. He was very conventional in his thinking. He provided Betty with the critical judgment that she lacked but would accept from him in the nonpersonal aspects of her life. She provided him with imagination and surprise, breaking his boredom and bringing excitement.

Let us summarize the characteristics of the predominantly analogic or digital coder on the level of cognition, problem-solving behavior, and clinical traits. (Of course, not all coders reach a high level of abstraction or of space-time integration.) A principally analogic coder of a low level of complexity and integration would be emotional, impulsive and without strategy, whereas a high-level analogic coder would be a strategist, quickly able to grasp totalities. A low-level digital coder would be stuck on the level of detail, having a command of facts but no real plan for solutions, whereas the high-level digital coder would be good at planning tactical action. Betty had a low level analogic coding style, whereas George had a high level digital style. Both the coding modes—digital or analogic—and the predominant level on which the subject thinks are important elements in the development of the thinking and learning style. One of the therapeutic objectives is to help the subject to achieve a "whole-brain" approach to his problem-solving thinking. His deficits must be diagnosed and corrected or compensated if he is to develop his potential for happiness by fulfilling his realistic conscious desire.

In Betty's case, the therapist helped her with the laborious task of developing an analytic space. He reframed her problem from one of maintaining a "holier-than-thou" image to one of anticipating the real consequences of her acts. The idea of having options, other than escape and trying to develop disciplined plans of action, were also dealt with. George was helped by the therapist's giving him explanations of why and how all human behavior is not motivated by logic. He was helped with his lack of empathy and of tolerance toward others, and his emotions were made apparent to him.

If we analyze the thinking and learning style of the Wolf Man, we find him to have been a predominantly analogic right-brain thinker functioning principally on middle levels of abstraction (integration), an experiential learner, and a person in whom strong affect reactions predominated over logical relations (Torrence 1984). Specifically, his interests were artistic and affect-oriented, not logical and achievement-oriented. He seems to have been interested in analogic symbolization, such as dreams and free associations. He was intuitive rather than analytic in thinking about such matters as the outcome of the Russian Revolution; it occurred to him suddenly that his fortune was in danger, but he had no logical reasons and no organized plan of action to go with the intuition. The affect-organized code took precedence over the logical code in the decision process. His decisions were influenced strongly by affect. His decision to marry Therese, for example, was based on the affect response to the discovery that she really cared for him. The logical impediments of class, religious, cultural, and educational differences and the consequences of social disapproval were of less importance.

Other characteristics of the Wolf Man, more typical of the right-brain personality, were his lifelong unfaithfulness, his leading of a double life, his undisciplined ways, his tendency to devalue others, his fear of solitude, and his failure to put his insights into practice. Also, he very frequently uses proverbs, stories, jokes, and examples in the conversations recorded by Obholzer (1982).

The thinking and learning style becomes another element of treatment to be taken into account in facilitating the subject's learning process and improving his capacity to achieve what he desires. Subjects with an analogic style, like the Wolf Man, tend to learn in response to concrete experience and example, whereas those with a more digital system learn more by instruction and logical explanation. We would expect the Wolf Man to have understand by experience rather than by explanation. The Wolf Man understood the need to take advantage of the treatment opportunity when this was made clear by Freud's actions. Freud set an arbitrary date for termination, and this made it clear to the Wolf Man that he must prepare himself by taking advantage of treatment. Words of interpretation had not been enough. Recall again the Wolf Man's insight that learning by remembering and talking is not enough: for him, it also had to be experienced in reality. He gave the following description of his own and Freud's perception of how he was to learn:

> And precisely in those matters in which I should be logical I fail. In theoretical matters I am logical. I would rather be logical where feelings are concerned. But it is interesting that he [Freud] should have said "don't

criticize, don't reflect, don't look for contradictions but accept what I tell you and improvement will come by itself" (Obholzer 1982:68)

We suggest that the Wolf Man probably learned by experiencing, but this does not obviate the necessity for his having evaluated the new experience critically. Even in experiential learners and in learning in which the purpose is the reorganization of the analogic system (learning that therefore must be experiential), the process must always involve both codes. The subject must elaborate and evaluate critically what has been learned. He cannot simply trust and obey. Much of what must be learned must be linked to the development of new projects and new plans of action. A further digital elaboration must take place if the fulfillment of the newly desirable is to be made possible. Cure involves the use of the complementary functions of the whole brain (Kagen and Kogan 1970). The Wolf Man's deficits included difficulty in making a plan of action, a lack of discipline in action, and a tendency to make decisions in response to affect without evaluating the real consequences. These difficulties should have been dealt with so that he could solve problems more effectively.

If we look for an example to contrast with the thinking style of the Wolf Man, we find it in the alexithymic—the operational thinker who reports no dreams or fantasies, is overconforming, and is unemotional in his decisions. This thinking style, which is left-hemispheric (Bogen 1975), manifests itself in a different series of problem-solving deficits. Such an individual, for example, does not capture the context in which events occur; he cannot anticipate another person's emotional reaction to his behavior; he is unable to form alliances; his planning is on the level of concrete operations; he gets bogged down in irrelevant detail; although overconforming, he is open to instruction; he can list existing options but cannot create new ones.

In summary, people can be classified in relation to the predominant style that characterizes their thinking and learning. There are two general parameters: coding mode and level of abstraction. The coding mode may be predominantly analogic as was that of the Wolf Man or predominantly digital as that of a patient who presents no dreams or fantasies and who seems divorced from his affect. The predominant thinking mode may be used principally on a low or high level of abstraction. Taking thinking and learning styles into account has therapeutic implications. It allows the analysand to learn to anticipate what his problem-solving deficits are likely to be. Therapeutic strategy may correct the deficit or try to compensate for it by selecting partners who are complementary in their functions.

11.
ANALOGIC CODING AND
COMPULSIVE DESIRE

In one sense, dual-coding theory coincides with Freud's thinking: it considers the analogic system more open in its ability to generate new possibilities and to create new connections *between* symbols, as in Freud's "free flow of energy." In another sense, however, it would consider the energy of primary process as excessively bound and operating under the compulsion principle. The subject is compelled to pursue certain historic goals with a strong emotional charge. The experience is *felt* in primary process when one symbolizes the early experience that organizes unconscious motivation. Here, the connection between the analogic symbol and the accompanying affect is especially strong, constant, direct, and beyond the reaches of reason or analysis; that is, it is excessively fixed and extremely difficult to reorganize. This overfixing of motivating energy is determined by two factors: the fact that the analogic code is affect-organized and the conditions in which this coding takes place (Gear and Liendo 1980).

As we have said, experiential evidence developed by Zajonc (1980) confirms that the relations to affect in the two symbolic systems are significantly distinct. In addition, the decision process in the analogic system is determined by the affect organization (like-dislike) given to experience, whereas in the digital mode the process represents reality and logic in relation to the probable result (Gear, Grinberg, and Liendo 1976).

Zanjonc (1980) demonstrated that human judgment obeys one of two independent processes. He suggests that left-hemispheric, digital, cognitive judgments are based on "discriminata"—that is, specific analyzable, logically connected component features of a stimulus. Affect judgments, however, are based on "preferenda," which are perceived holistically, understood synthetically, and organized by the affect "like-dislike" with which the experience has been registered. The distinction between the processes becomes evident in the speed with which the subject arrives at the affect conclusion; the logical conclusion is reached much more slowly. The affect category has been determined and the decision has been made before the subject is even consciously aware that he has had previous experience with the stimulus and long before logical discrimination and analysis are made. We would take this contrast as confirmation that the analogic system is affect-organized, whereas the digital system is affect-linked but organized by logic. If the affect experience unit is coded without logic, it is apparent that it cannot be changed by the application of logical analysis alone.

In addition, the conditions under which the early interpersonal experience is coded tend to create a strong sense of conviction, which increases even further the difficulty in changing the historic motivation. This early interpersonal experience is not only coded analogically and often a product of the preverbal phase; it is lived in the conditions that Bruner (1973) describes as producing a strongly held hypothesis. The experience being coded has a strong emotional impact: it is of vital importance; it is strongly rewarded or punished; it is repeated frequently in circumstances in which only one understanding is offered, and this understanding is shared with the most significant others. This strong relationship between the historic experience and the vital implications of the agreeable or disagreeable emotion results in a further bonding between the affect and the experience. A great emotional conviction develops in relation to such experience, and this gives further permanence to meaning. It can be said that the emotional cost of change is high and that the subject cannot or will not pay this price. Therefore, he goes back to the old solutions, rigidly maintaining his obsolete historic paradigm.

The reorganization of affect is especially difficult in these analogically coded, preverbal, affect-bound hypotheses (bonding), which constitute the group of experiences coded in conditions of the strongly held hypothesis. Such experiences form the basis for development of the subject's interpersonal paradigm and the accompanying melodramatic, sadomasochistic interpersonal game. Although the subject's conscious, analytic, and reality-evaluating functions permit him to develop other possibilities in the interpersonal realm, he is not involved deeply or committed emotionally to these possibilities, which are permitted *theoretically* by freer, more evolved actual circumstances. We suggest that unconscious and (to a certain degree) conscious motivation are bound by the strength of the historic conviction derived from this primary affect-experience unit, lived in the circumstances described by Bruner. Therefore, the subject develops a strong motivation to seek a certain class of experience and to avoid that class that historically was feared so strongly. Symbolic change implies facing rather than defending against the historic anxiety. The immediate price is high but the long-term gain is great.

At the age of eighty, the Wolf Man had not given up his sadomasochistic interpersonal game of superiority-inferiority, in which he sought to establish relations with inferior women whom he used, devalued, and, at the same time, maintained in order to have the power to play his abusive game. In this way, he wished to recreate the sensation of being the favored child, loved, and valued in a special way by his father (Gear and Liendo 1979). He also wished to avoid the catastrophic sensation of devaluation and profound rejection that he suffered when he lost this favored position to his sister. He could not face the anxiety; therefore, he could not resolve the problem of his lack of personal development.

When his compulsive behavior failed to produce the sensation of superiority and of the consequent continued favor that he so needed, the Wolf Man was confronted with a second set of disquieting emotions, which defeated further any real effort to develop himself. His rage toward his powerful father was very frightening to him because it could produce a counterattack. This fear of his own destructive anger resulted in a paralysis of normal aggression and an excessively passive and submissive attitude toward authority figures. This attitude also persisted until the age of eighty!

The Wolf Man's fear of inferiority made him pass his time in defensive action, which perpetuated the very insecurities against which it defended. His fear of the consequences of his envious aggression also prevented his personal development, which would have reduced the reason for his envy.

The Wolf Man suffered a motivational compulsion—the repetition compulsion described by Freud (1914)—and the divalence between unconscious compulsion and conscious desire described by us (Gear and Liendo 1979). The motivation compulsion was to repeat the sadomasochistic interpersonal game of inferiority-superiority. The conscious motivation would have been to be loved for himself and his qualities; his unconscious defensive motivation would have been to escape from the unpleasant feeling of inferiority and the threat of rejection and abandonment by devaluing the other. The analysis of the two affect-experience units, "inferiority-rejection" and "aggressive rage-destruction," is essential to the resolution of the divalence between the conscious desire to have been loved for himself and the unconscious defensive desire to have avoided the threat of inferiority feelings by selecting socioeconomically inferior women as partners, whom he could devalue because of their dependence. These units had to have been broken for desire to be freed from its sadomasochistic constriction. That is, the Wolf Man had to have faced his actual inferiority, or, more properly, his arrest in development, and have recognized that he would not have been rejected for it. He should have felt valued for his effort and safe enough to make the effort if he were to develop his own potential.

This step, modifying the affect organizers of the deep unconscious, is the depth analysis that Freud (1912) considered so important when he argued that it was necessary to arrive at the early traumatic experience of the subject: to put it into words, to label it, and to bring it into consciousness. We would add that the analysand must pay the price by facing his anxiety, living and experiencing emotionally the new, relevant, and therapeutic interpersonal and socioeconomic relationship (Gear, Liendo, and Scott 1983). In such a relationship, the Wolf Man would have been respected and encouraged in his efforts to develop himself and discouraged from his defensive choice of inferior women, whom he had to devalue in an effort to prove them worthless. In simple terms, he should have been encouraged to invest in production, not in defense. He should have given up the defensive game of distributing unhappiness unfairly and begun to play the game of producing happiness for himself and others (Gergen, Greenberg, and Willis 1980).

Such a change would be essential to the passage from the defensive, melodramatic, avoided desire, most evident in anxiety states, to a dramatic productive desire for happiness, which appears in states of psychic competence. The avoided desire of *no anxiety* is fulfilled by sacrificing the desire for happiness. The desire for happiness is achieved by confronting certain unavoidable states of anxiety. This is simply the price of growth.

Passing conceptually (that is, through intellectual insight) from the desire for *no anxiety* to the desire for *happiness* is not sufficient in itself. There must also be a simultaneous analogic passage from the traumatic experience to the experience of satisfactory competence. The change is experiential as well as theoretical, and it exacts a high cost in immediately experienced anxiety. In contrast, the defense costs little in the short run; anxiety is avoided, but the long-term cost is high. The subject tends to invest his resources very strongly in defense and to neglect projects that produce happiness.

THERAPEUTIC IMPLICATIONS

These propositions about the relationship of affect to understanding have important implications in the therapeutic process. The reorganization of conscious motivation and the logical relations to affect can be achieved by a logical analysis, whereas the reorganization of unconscious motivation and of the historic relations to affect requires a consistent corrective experiencing of a nonmelodramatic interpersonal relationship. It does not respond simply to a logical analysis. Therefore, we agree with Freud that transference must be analyzed as it is experienced to be truly understood. We would add, however, that a new relationship must also be identified and experienced if transference is to be resolved as well as understood. The experiencing of that which was specifically necessary and which was excluded historically is required to free desire from its sadomasochistic compulsion. In other words, what *was present*—the affect-experiential understanding given by the father and that given by the mother—is not enough. Whas *was not* within the constricting frame—the nonmelodramatic, nonsadomasochistic interpersonal relationship relevant to healthy productive motivation—must actually be given in experience to the subject. It must be modeled; it must be labeled, analyzed, and *felt*. This is the corrective and enriching experience usually represented but not signified (no affect meaning) in the potential unconscious. It is specifically necessary to free the affect-experience bonded deep unconscious. The affect-experience unit produced a conviction about the melodramatic and sadomasochistic relation between self and others, as if this were the only relationship possible rather than the source of the problem. The analogic affect-bonded representation resides in the deep unconscious and is unique to the analogic primary process, where experience and affect were lived as an inseparable and unanalyzable unit.

The analogic aspects of therapy—the therapeutic setting and the real, paratransferential interpersonal relationship—become, therefore, the important elements in actually reorganizing affect in the bonded units. The analogic experience is necessary for the freeing of desire. The digital, logical analysis is correspondingly essential in the attempts at fulfilling this freed and enriched desire.

Digital secondary process is organized by the development of logical relations among symbols. In secondary process, the affect is secondary to the logical relations between symbols and to the logical evaluation given to the experience. The affect link results from a realistic analysis of possible outcomes, risks, and probabilities. Therefore, decisions for action are made in relation to conscious desire rather than on the grounds of the affect-bonded, constricting, irrelevant, sadomasochistic convictions of childhood. Changing the conscious relation to affect is a much easier task because it takes place as a result of the use of analytic and logical techniques. The changing of the deep unconscious motivation takes place only with difficulty and at a high cost because it entails consistently lived corrective experience.

III

REFRAMING PATHOLOGY AND THERAPY

12.
TECHNIQUES FOR FREEDOM
AND HAPPINESS

As therapists, our concern is to help the analysand free himself from the repetition compulsion and from the traumatic incompetence that keeps him from fulfilling his conscious desire for happiness. We seek to help him to pass from an avoidant, defensive role, occupied with the unfair distribution of unhappiness, to a confronting, productive role in which he is free to enhance happiness for himself and others. To do this, we diagnose in what sense the analysand acts unproductively and how his performance could be modified. We deal with the working through of the defensive melodrama. We address the working out and correction of the deficits which have made the traumatic incompetence and dramatic failure inevitable. And we explore the breaking through of the constrictions of the paradigm to incorporate representations from the potential unconscious.

We believe that mental health is characterized by the freedom to pursue happiness, whereas the mentally ill pursue compulsively the unconscious goal of distributing unhappiness unfairly through the reenactment of their escapist melodrama. They are unable to contain their anxiety enough to confront a dramatic and extremely threatening incompetence. The incompetence has caused a failure in relation to a vitally important problem. The melodrama diverts attention from the dramatic problem and the underlying incompetence. The drama is rarely referred to in the clinical material or is mentioned as if incidental and unimportant. This threat of vital failure, which results from deficits on the conceptual, emotional, or operational level, brings the defenses into operation. It is not sufficient for the therapist simply to diagnose these deficits and defenses. Deficits must be either corrected or supplemented on the level on which they occur, and the defenses against major and minor anxieties must be overcome. In addition, the affect and social resistances that organize motivation and make change difficult must be dealt with as they reinforce the narrow and inadequate paradigm and perpetuate the unconscious compulsion.

The analysand and his therapist are joined in a conscious alliance to address these problems and to improve the effectiveness of efforts to free and fulfill desire. To accompany his patient toward these objectives, the therapist has as a major resource a systematic and effective technology derived from his theoretical models (Argyris and Schon 1974).

DREAM FULFILLMENT AS THE GOAL OF THERAPY

We define happiness as the affect state that results from the fulfillment of productive desire. The broad purpose of therapy is the fulfillment of the subject's realistic desire for happiness. This requires the freeing of desire from compulsion, the enrichment of desire by the inclusion of the newly desirable from the potential unconscious, and, finally, the problem-solving thinking and action necessary to fulfill this free and healthier desire.

This definition allows us to determine seven progressive steps in therapy. The first is related to the short-term goal of reducing the level of traumatic anxiety by rebalancing the system in its normal way of functioning. It also entails making a strategic diagnosis to determine the sequence of therapeutic tasks and operations and the real possibility of achieving them within the resources committed to this project. The second stage is related to resolving the melodramatic defense and reverting the inverted identity. In this stage the resistances to be overcome are minor. Third, the drama is faced and worked out. This implies correcting the defensive displacement and correcting or compensating the deficits that have created the predisposition to the vital failure. A fourth stage is related to breaking the frame constrictions to include the repudiated, those *extra-frame* representations that are actively excluded from the *intraframe* spaces. Here the potential for happiness is increased as the analysand develops the emotional competence to analyze his traumatic incompetence, thus releasing desire from compulsion. A fifth and long-term goal is to enrich the *intraframe* spaces with the *extraframe* creative potential. The release of desire from its defensive occupation with the distribution of unhappiness allows the subject to imagine new projects for happiness, if his potential unconscious is adequately developed. As a sixth step, a corresponding environmental change is required as the subject experiences a change in his understanding, desire, and performance. Others should be sought who share and reinforce his paradigm. They become allies in mental health, rather than accomplices in illness. This implies a further seventh step in which the imagined is put into action. A concrete project and plan for dream fulfillment is developed, taking into account the resources and limitations of the analysand.

DEFICITS, DEFENSES, AND RESISTANCES IN ANALYSIS

Just as it appears in relations with the analysand's significant others, unproductive and counterproductive performance also appears in the therapeutic task related to deficits, resistances, and defenses. These must be managed and overcome gradually in the therapeutic process. Having defined psychopathology as an imprisoning compulsive motivation to distribute unhappiness unfairly, we will now define deficits, defenses, and resistances so that they can be linked to therapeutic strategy and technique.

We define a deficit as that which is absent or deficient in thought and action on the conceptual, emotional, instrumental, and biological level. Deficits predispose the subject to the vital failure and the crisis of competence for which he consults. A deficit may be universal, such as narrowness, causal simplification, and polarization, or specific, as seen in coding style and in the related conceptual capacity for problem-solving. In addition, specific deficits may exist on the operational level in the organization and execution of problem-solving performance. Necessary operational skills may be lacking.

We will use the case of Betty as an example. Betty had the following universal conceptual deficits. She did not include an understanding and empathic relationship within the expected possibilities of interpersonal relations. The narrowness of her paradigm omitted this vital material from her *intraframe* symbolic system. Her causal simplification was manifest in her attributing all difficulties in understanding to the other who, like her mother, simply wouldn't understand. Others were polarized into categories of those who misunderstood and those who were misunderstood. Her specific conceptual deficits included her coding style, which was analogic and deficient in digito-logical functions. She did not elaborate her thoughts but acted on impulse with very little consideration for real or long-term consequences. She was unable to think about her own understanding. She could not analyze problems, nor could she organize a series of actions that would bring her closer to a desired result. She lacked skills in the socioeconomic sphere where she was overprotected by her husband. On an emotional level, Betty was unable to contain her own anxiety. Nor was she open enough to easily permit help.

Defense is against anxiety; it is an important factor in the perpetuation of pathology. The defenses may be categorized as those against the anxiety of recognizing the dramatic event that precipitated the vital failure (defensive displacement to the melodrama); those against the anxiety of recognizing true identity (defensive inversion of identity); those against the anxiety of recognizing the failure of a fundamental, socially shared paradigm (anxiety provoked by recognition that the game must be changed). Defensive inversion results from the action of four mechanisms. The true identity is repressed into the unconscious; it is identified projectively in the other; the other introjects and denies the introjection. It is a defense requiring the complicity of a complementary other. Thus, the accomplice must be taken into account in the process of cure. In therapy, attempts must be made to convert him into an ally of healthy performance instead of an accomplice in the defensive escape to the melodrama.

From the point of view of her defense, Betty repeated a melodramatic angry response to any communication that questioned her, using her aggression to avoid an honest confrontation with inadequate social behavior. She failed to recognize her own lack of understanding, her arbitrary and aggressive treatment toward the therapist and her husband. She projected this lack of understanding on others and identified herself as the one not understood. She did not examine the paradigm of her family game, which was held with great conviction in her family of origin. The rules of this game were: "Letting the other find out is what gets you into trouble. Being caught, not what you do, is what is dangerous." Honest communication was repudiated, and she was trapped within her limiting frame.

Resistance is resistance to change. Because change implies, among other things, the confrontation of incongruences that have been recognized as such, the avoidant melodramatic defenses must be resolved if change is to take place. Change also depends on resources, on significant others, and on the formation of alliances with these others. That is, resistance to change (or the facilitation of change, for that matter) entails a personal, an environmental, and a power aspect as well as a symbolic aspect. Therefore, the reinforcing social environment is an important source of resistance. Resistances are reflected in the continued acting of the melodrama and the environmental pressure (which comes from the group that shares and confirms the paradigm) to continue to act in this stereotyped, compulsive way. Environmental resistances could be said to be generated by the analysand as he selects, induces, and reinforces an environment that is in complicity with his pathological paradigm. The environment becomes an independent, active, and powerful perpetrator of the illness. It does not simply dissolve when the analysand becomes desirous of another, more healthy milieu.

In Betty's case, she did not analyze her assumptions, she acted. She was confirmed in her deeply feared worthlessness by the lover whom she chose. He humiliated and used her and later denounced her. She had developed a series of friendships with promiscuous and psychopathic individuals from whom she could obtain a sense of comaraderie by acting out sexually. Fortunately, her husband was not a part of the reinforcing environment. He could forgive her only when she was able to recognize the seriousness of what she had done. She herself was defensively aggressive toward her husband. This was a pathogenic factor that tended to interrupt the communication and perpetuate the melodrama.

OVERCOMING EMOTIONAL INCOMPETENCE

In moments of crisis, the cognitive incongruence and the threat of psychic chaos, as well as a pragmatic failure in a vital area, combine in the person to produce a traumatic level of anxiety, as opposed to a signal level. A signal level of anxiety would be met with healthy problem-solving behavior. In this case, the anxiety calls attention to the need for change, and the subject analyzes the unresolved *problem* on the level of symbolization, conceptualization, and operations. In addition, he analyzes frame defenses against the anxiety of moral or cognitive incongruence and chaotic disorganization. Within the frame, he analyzes the defensive inversion to avoid the unpleasant recognition of this identity. The ability to face anxiety and to contain it is called "emotional competence." Without this ability, the analysand experiences a traumatic level of anxiety and becomes defensive. Helping the analysand to deal with his anxiety and to confront his dramatic incompetence is an important function of the therapist. It requires that the level be reduced through compensation of the failing system. The therapist transmits congruence, stability, and the disposition to accompany the analysand in his quest for freedom.

In Betty's case, if the anxiety had been signal, she would have recognized that her problem was impulsive self-destructive acting, not being caught. She would have seen her actions as incongruent with her own conscious desire to be loved and her definition of acceptable behavior. She would have identified her husband as someone loving her in spite of her imperfections, willing to "understand" and to help her to deal with the destructive part of herself. Her own emotional capacity was insufficient to allow her to face her problems.

Traumatic anxiety, on the other hand, is met with a defense that then perpetuates the underlying failure. Here, the *anxiety itself* has been taken as the problem rather than as a signal that a real dramatic problem exists and must be resolved. The defensive subject has opted to reduce immediate anxiety instead of facing and dealing with the vital dramatic problem. He cannot pay the immediate emotional price of growth and is left with a long-term payment, in which he mortgages his resources for future happiness (Cook and Emerson 1978).

Betty suffered traumatic anxiety and escaped from a recognition of her own inadequate behavior by taking the problem as one of having been caught because a lover betrayed her. She did not face and deal with her own anxiety provoked by her tendency to act impulsively. She failed to evaluate the destructive consequences of her behavior. She did not mention her traumatic anxiety, related to a sense of worthlessness, and her boredom with her unproductive life until much later in therapy. She initially failed to identify and to address the dramatic incompetence.

INTRAFRAME DRAMA AND MELODRAMA, *EXTRAFRAME* SOLUTION

On the level of coding, mental illness is linked to what is *already* a part of the constricted conscious space and how this is distorted and maintained.

What is *intraframe* also includes what is already a part of the equally constricted content of the unconscious. The *intraframe* is selected, organized, and constricted by the preconscious paradigm. Dissonant *extraframe* information, in contrast, cannot be integrated into the subject's knowledge without a change in the frame convictions because this *extraframe* repudiated information is not consonant with the assumptions in their valuative and cognitive aspects (Deutsch, Krass, and Rosneau 1962). That is, it lies *outside* these limits in the potential unconscious and is actively selected out and rejected from entry into the *intraframe* spaces. In the new focus that this model brings, a key therapeutic task is to overcome frame defenses and to integrate the *extraframe* dissonant information from the potential unconscious.

In the case of the Wolf Man, there are easily distinguishable *intraframe* and *extraframe* tasks that should have been taken up. Inside the frame, the Wolf Man signified his role in the interpersonal melodrama of the "superior-inferior" social and family game. Within the unquestioned constrictions of the "superior-inferior" game, in his conscious space, he simply distorted (inverted) information about who was "superior" and who was "inferior." The direct perception of himself as "inferior" and the accompanying unpleasantness of confirming this perception were present within the frame but repressed; they were represented in the superficial layers of the unconscious (Gear, Liendo, and Scott 1983).

In the Wolf Man's potential unconscious were games directed at the production of happiness, but these were not motivating. The unconscious affect that organizes compulsive unconscious motivation was cathected to the game of "superior-inferior," where the one who was "inferior" had to suffer an unfair amount of displeasure. The *intraframe* task would have been one of reverting the inverted identity within the melodramatic game. Especially in a crisis of competence, when the unconscious traumatic fear of the vital incompetence was reactivated, the Wolf Man was limited to his historic problem space. He understood the problem that should have been solved as that of distributing the displeasure related to being inferior. But the dramatic problem that precipitated the crisis was not addressed, and the production of happiness became impossible. The constricted conscious problem-solving space used interpersonal and politicoeconomic power and resources to establish blame or inferiority. Power was at the service of this distribution task. In a healthy state, the tools for power are seen as useful for the production of happiness and not simply as instruments for the distribution of unhappiness (Emerson 1962).

The Wolf Man's case reveals the importance of this constriction in the type of game that is articulated to the preconscious frame and is linked emotionally to the deep unconscious. He was not convinced—that is, he lacked the emotional conviction—that he *could* play a game productive of interpersonal happiness, in which he could make contributions to common projects for happiness. He was unable to think about a game in which a fair share of self-worth and pleasure was felt while happiness was produced with the energy and resources at hand. Representations of these games were not incorporated, but stayed in the *extraframe* potential unconscious. In such cases, representations like these are beyond frame constrictions and outside the conscious problem-solving space. In addition, they do not form a part of the early experience that is bonded to the affect organizers of the psychic system. They are not motivating. Their becoming signified within the *intraframe* spaces is an important focus of therapy, as understood from our theoretical position.

The *intraframe* problem may be resolved by analytic techniques such as interpretation of transference. The *extraframe* problem requires a new, consistently lived therapeutic learning experience, reinforced within the therapeutic environment. The therapeutic setting reframes the analysand's frame. It acts to pressure him to change his assumptions. If the therapist is reframed within the analysand's assumptions, rather than challanging them, the therapist becomes ill rather than the analysand becoming healthy.

In Betty's case, for instance, she signified her role as that of a good misunderstood victim, unjustly and indiscriminately accused by a bad misunderstanding mother. The direct perception of herself as misunderstanding and unjustly accusing was within the frame but was repressed in the superficial layer of the unconscious.

Outside the frame was a totally new game directed at producing happiness to be shared with understanding others. When this possibility was included within the problem space and became motivating, a second order change took place. To achieve such a change requires that *extraframe* dissonant material become a part of the framing assumptions. This meets with a major degree of resistance. Betty's efforts had been directed at avoiding the other's discovery and accusation. The dramatic problem of doing something that she herself deemed worthy of respect and positive attention was not addressed. The *intraframe* task had to do with reverting her inverted perception of identity. The *extraframe* task had to do with freeing her to play another, more productive game. In addition

TECHNIQUES FOR FREEDOM AND HAPPINESS

to an analysis of transference, it required a structuring of a new nontransferential relationship within the therapeutic situation and with her husband, then with the members of the larger community. Betty had to identify, live, and experience affectively this relationship in order for it to be integrated into her system of understanding and motivation.

BREAKING THROUGH THE SELF-SEALING FRAME

All subjects are limited in the dimensions of their understanding by the narrowness of their experience. What is pathological, however, is not the narrowness represented in this limitation, but the dogmatic constricting reinforcement of this narrowness. Idealization of what is valuatively consonant and denigration of what is valuatively dissonant are the frame mechanisms through which change is resisted. These processes seal the frame from within, making it impermeable to the enriching information from the potential unconscious.

In addition, the cognitively consonant is perceived as the natural and only way to think. Of course, the existence of the cognitive set itself is not pathological: a cognitive set always exists when a person learns from past experience. However, when the cognitive set is taken as the only and natural way, there is no search for new possibilities.

The defensive rigidity and impermeability of the frame become important problems in therapeutic transformation. They are responsible for the pathologically closed mind, which is both old *and* fixed in its understanding. Rigidity can be equated to resistance, because even after the information has penetrated the frame, the action paradigm persists in the face of recognized failure or inadequacy.

The resistance of the paradigm to change is also related to its *social* origin and to the conditions in which it is learned. The paradigm is derived from the underlying valuative, cognitive, and identity assumptions, socially held and taught in a way that strongly rewards its acceptance and strongly punishes its rejection to the point of threatening survival. This produces the strength of affect commitment with which the paradigm is held and the consequent tendency to rigidity and closure (Asch 1952).

Betty assumed—and this was confirmed in the community in which she grew up—that sexual behavior was bad. Sexual play had been punished very severely when it was discovered. She was very inhibited in her sexual behavior in her marriage. Betty also shared a conviction that attack followed discovery, a conviction held by her family and valid in her childhood environment. Her mother, in fact, attacked and accused, with or without justification.

The Wolf Man shared with his environment the assumption that his aristocratic birth gave him protection and privilege. This was a socially shared assumption, historically valid at the time that it was learned. His state of privilege did exist, and it was generally accepted as natural by significant others such as his father and his Nanya as well as also being shared and reinforced strongly by his society at that time.

The Wolf Man, however, persisted rigidly in this assumption even after it had become clearly invalid. Although his forced migration and the loss of his fortune represented dramatic changes in his social environment, he could not make the corresponding change in his paradigm, thus confirming that "you can take a man out of his culture more readily that you can take the culture out of a man." He tended to remain firmly fixed on this strong emotionally cathected fundamental assumption. He did, of course, accept the need to earn his daily bread, and he finally accepted an offer for work. Therese supported him in this move, and he gave her credit for his constancy in this effort. He seems to have worked, however without a sense of pleasure or self-realization. He continued to use economic power as a source of superiority toward others, especially after Therese's death, when once again he entered a crisis of competence and reverted sharply to his old family game. Even in his later years, he still regarded it as natural that Freud had taken up a collection for him for seven years. He could not understand Mack Brunswick's criticism of this action; he had simply persisted in his feeling of a right to social privilege.

In the Wolf Man's history, the aristocratic class had been idealized even when it was inept and unproductive, whereas the lower class was denigrated even when it was productive, although uncultured. These were not simply narrow assumptions to be modified readily after new experience. Any attempt to change these ideas was likely to bring a dogmatic disqualification against the lucid critic of society. Such an observer was likely to be disqualified as an inferior or a bad revolutionary. The general environment accepted and shared these assumptions actively to the point where they could not be changed readily on a social level, even when their pragmatic failure was evident. The society resorted to a battle of physical forces in order to impose change.

The Russian Revolution did not really change these concepts. Even for the revolutionaries, it was easier to attack the aristocrats than to change the paradigm to a productive orientation. Privilege merely changed hands, from the aristocrats to the members of the Politburo. The roles in the game were simply inverted, but the problem continued to be oriented toward the distribution of displeasure; now it was forced upon the aristocrats. We suggest that on the public as well as the personal level, an alteration in the game from distributive concerns to productivity is more difficult than a revolution, which is often simply a forced reversion of roles and falls short of a change on the level of the game.

On the individual level, a challenge to the frame assumptions brings real pressure from the others who also live by those assumptions and who are a principal source of resistance to a mutation. Rejection, disqualification, withholding rewards, actively punishing or ignoring the other—all can be used as pressures to conformity, to make the person return to the socially shared understanding. This fact is exemplified in the resistance that the Wolf Man met when he decided to violate the social rules and to marry Therese, rather than to exploit her sexually. He stated that a woman who did not speak French would be rejected immediately by his social peers, regardless of any personal qualities and certainly regardless of Therese's excellent record of honesty, devotion to duty, and social usefulness. As a life partner, Therese was unacceptable to Kraeplin, his mother, and his friends (Deutsch 1975). Only Freud, who came from another culture and who had a therapeutic perspective on the special dynamic problems that the Wolf Man had to resolve, appreciated her personal worth and her special value to the Wolf Man. Therefore, he supported the Wolf Man in his plans to marry her. This, incidentally, is the reason that the Wolf Man gave for staying in treatment with Freud. Freud's judgment went beyond the cultural and family frame constrictions. He demonstrated his *extraframe* metalucidity.

A healthy, flexible individual holds assumptions that he recognizes as assumptions. That is, he perceives them as shared assumptions that are socially determined and limited rather than natural, correct, or superior. The assumptions may be made conscious without any great resistance. The Wolf Man was certainly aware of what he assumed; his resistance was related to *changing* the assumptions. That is, inevitable preconscious frame narrowness became pathologically constricting as a result of frame resistances combined with the social pressures of a pathogenic consensus. To modify the frame requires *extraframe* metalucidity to perceive it objectively from outside its constrictions, an *extraframe* (potential unconscious) capacity to develop options that lie outside the constrictions, and power to overcome the forces of resistance to change.

The Wolf Man's therapist first had to have the lucidity to see the defensive melodramatic interpersonal game as a learned and shared set of social assumptions, which were neither natural nor productive of happiness and which had to be questioned. In such a case, the therapist assumes an auxiliary creative signifying function as he helps to explore the potential unconscious and to offer an alternate paradigm of understanding, in which contribution and retribution are related and in which value is given to the relevant dramatic problems to be overcome for the production of happiness.

The person's philosophy of life is being studied. In the case of mental illness, this seems to be limited principally to distributing unhappiness in a sadomasochistic way. It is from the potential unconscious that a philosophy and corresponding paradigm can be developed. To give the message a therapeutic impact, the therapist must have power: authority, persuasive capacity, technical resources, the potential for rewarding and sanctioning (revaluing) in order to pressure the analysand to incorporate his insight and redefinitions into his theory. If the confirming environment (significant others) is more powerful that the therapist, the analysand will be unable to achieve a change. The price of change rises sharply when it is punished by the environment. Thus, the Wolf Man's continued relationship with Luise influenced his behavior more powerfully than any therapeutic endeavor.

The force of the environment and significant others should not be underestimated in developing a therapeutic strategy. Therapeutic alliance with others is not limited to the therapeutic setting. Consensus and confirmation in the environment are important therapeutic forces. Power and consensus are as important as lucidity and creativity if the new design for life is to go beyond the drawing board.

In Betty's case, it was crucial to include her husband and to help him to react in a way that invalidated Betty's assumptions about being pursued and not being understood. She strongly induced a countertransferential response of accusations and attack. Her immediate environment contained some psychopathic and perverse individuals who carried out lives of distrust and insincerity. To change, it was important to select a new environment with a new set of friends, open, honest and nonaccusatory. Action, as it occurs in the therapeutic setting and in the environment, is a force often more powerful than words.

13.
RESISTANCE TO CHANGE:
A SOCIAL AND EMOTIONAL
PROBLEM

To clarify our understanding of therapeutic technique regarding resistance (in contrast to deficits and defenses) and to make clear the importance that this model gives to affect, environment, power, and the action mode, as well as to simple verbal presentation of corrective and enriching information, we will briefly review Freud's consideration (1895) of resistance to therapeutic change. In his efforts to develop a technique to deal with this problem, he tried hypnosis, abreaction, and, finally, free association. His early understanding of resistance demonstrates that he occupied himself originally with resistance to making conscious that which was repressed in the unconscious. He related the affect charge to the degree of resistance that could be expected. The subject's resistance was analyzed in "layers" until that which was most deeply buried could be made conscious. That which was considered to produce the most negative affect when uncovered was what Freud believed to be most deeply and strongly repressed and most resistant to being made conscious.

We agree with Freud that affect is indeed an important factor in the strength of resistance. This affect charge, however, is not related exclusively to that which is repressed in the deep unconscious. Many aspects of the preconscious paradigm are held with strong degrees of conviction, such as the social understanding of the games to be played, identity, and the rules of morality. That is, the concepts consciously held with conviction, or the "strongly held hypotheses" of Jerome Bruner (1973), as well as the motivating affect of the deep unconscious, are sources of resistance to change. The change itself is not simply a symbolic reorganization; it is

126

a symbolic enrichment and implies a transactional social process that obeys power considerations.

The same kind of rethinking of resistance seems to have influenced Freud (1923) when he formulated his second topical model of ego, id, and superego. He related resistance in his new topical model to five manifestations: he defined three ego resistances—repression, transference, and secondary gain; one unconscious resistance—the unconscious motivation to the repetition compulsion; and one superego resistance—the tendency to judge morally and to blame and punish the attempts at change.

In our proposed model, we attache importance to Freud's original idea that the resistance is related to the degree of affect involved in the concept to be changed. As we have stated, the social pressures and the socially shared nature of paradigms may produce strong affect conviction. Affect is involved with the unquestioned and idealized framing assumptions, which are shared socially in the conditions in which they are learned. The rewarding of shared belief, for example, is an important source of resistance to a change.

To change, the subject must pay a social price. We attribute great importance to the mechanisms that operate on the level of the frame and to those social forces exerted by the significant other and by the general social environment. They are the forces largely responsible for the difficulty in achieving changes. Because the lucid informer is usually disqualified from within the frame constrictions, power considerations are strategic if the information is to be accepted. The therapist must develop power (power of authority, of status, of special knowledge, of alliances) as well as possess the lucidity to overcome the forces of resistance (Marx 1963).

In the case of Betty, the therapist, who was perceived as having expert knowledge, was able to form a therapeutic alliance with the husband. At one moment when Betty was convinced that the therapist was like her mother, wanting to accuse and blame, she questioned his motives with a friend who was a former patient. The friend formed a therapeutic consensus by confirming the therapist's reputation as a serious and concerned professional. The therapeutic power was reinforced by the lucid witnesses, the husband and friend. Thus, the therapeutic setting had been successfully extended to include the family and friends.

The therapeutic setting is vital. The analysand's frame is reframed in therapy and in the environment. If the therapist accepts the analysand's frame, the therapist will become contaminated by the analysand's pathology and will lose his own mental health rather than achieving a cure. For instance, if the analyst permits the analysand to miss appointments or to fail to pay the sum that has been specified, the analyst is accepting abuse and may become depressed while the analysand's illness is reinforced.

MAJOR AND MINOR ANXIETIES AND RESISTANCES

To make the analysand conscious of his constricting assumptions has been found clinically to be easier on the level of inverted identity than on the level of the game itself. That is, it would have been easier for the Wolf Man to perceive his own powerlessness and inferiority than to recognize that producing happiness is the relevant objective. That this kind of perception is easier is to be expected because the problem of inverted identity can be addressed with information that already exists in the *intraframe* unconscious space, whereas the problem of changing the game requires the introduction of dissonant *extraframe* information from the potential unconscious.

The Wolf Man was familiar with and able to assume the role of the devalued and abused character in the family game, as with his sister and later with Luise. Or, if he was powerful enough to make the choice, he assumed the preferred role of the abusive and devaluing personage. The inversion of roles was familiar to him. On the level of his concepts and his motivation to action, however, the idea of *not playing* the irrelevant defensive melodramatic game of privileged superior and underprivileged inferior was much more difficult to achieve. Generally, changing roles produces displeasure; change in the game produces panic. The Wolf Man seems to have remained convinced that the relevant question in the game of life was *who* was to suffer the displeasure of devaluing humiliation and affect abandonment, which was the fate of the one who was defined as inferior. It is so difficult to change the historic melodramatic game the Wolf Man had regressed to after Therese's death and was still playing sixty years after his first analysis. His mental health was a shared dymanic state. When he lost Therese, he lost his balance again, and, in his crisis of confidence, he returned to the mechanisms of his childhood.

Betty could more readily accept that she was the one who did not understand and who was unjustly accusatory to her husband and analyst than accept that this game was itself unnecessarily limited to unhealthy and unhappy possibilities. It was difficult to get her to accept the understanding and acceptance of the other as sincere. She thought that everyone divided the world into the pure and perfect "Pollyannas" or the impure and sexually promiscuous. She took relationships of dishonesty as natural and did not question them. She also consistently made a dogmatic disqualification of the other when he made an effort to show understanding. He was taken to be a dishonest "Pollyanna," pretending to be a good understanding friend while really being secretly accusing.

DOGMATISM: A SOURCE OF RESISTANCE

The dogmatic resistance of the frame, which we consider the most difficult of the resistances, is somewhat analogous to Freud's idea of the superego resistance. This resistance, however, does not always use Freud's mechanism of blame as its tool for power. We consider the characteristic devaluation of those who hold different views and the idealization of socially shared beliefs as the most generalized dogmatic mechanisms. We also find that certain cultures and families emphasize one of the mechanisms—blaming or devaluing—over the other. In the case of the Wolf Man, resistance was the result of dogmatic devaluation. Therese, for example, who encouraged him to develop himself at the university and to face his economic need to work, was devalued strongly by his family and his social group (and by the Wolf Man himself, for that matter). Her advice was perceived as having little weight. Her lucidity lacked social power. Therapy takes power considerations into account to overcome dogmatism. The power to influence the environment or to remove the analysand from it is often key to achieving a lasting positive change.

TRANSFERENCE AND COUNTERTRANSFERENCE IN RESISTANCE

Transference resistance is reinforced when the analysand manages to induce a countertransferential reaction in the therapist that confirms his perspective. He does not simply act instead of analyzing; he also confirms successfully in action the pragmatic validity of his paradigm, thereby reinforcing his belief and successfully avoiding the need for real change; his paradigm, far from failing, is strongly confirmed. For instance, Betty was very successful in inspiring a lack of trust in her husband. This was a strong induction for him to pursue and accuse her. Her suppositions were made valid by her own actions.

The therapist must quickly identify the pressures that induce him to accept and act out the countertransferential role. This role is not simply projected onto him; it is identified projectively and induced actively. The transference resistance is not solved only by an analysis of its cognitive content. Resolution depends on consistent realistic disconfirmation. This is only possible if the therapist successfully avoids the countertransferential role and consistently introduces a new type of relationship that is specifically focused on resolving the dilemma. The therapeutic setting needs to include action. The therapist must counter the patient's choice between the father's action and that of the mother with real choices from among options represented in the potential unconscious space. In this way, the therapist not only avoids a countertransferential counter acting-out but also designs and introduces a specific therapeutic relationship to solve the dilemma of the false choice. The historic options do not allow solutions adequate to today's problems. Even less do they permit the development of potential. The therapeutic reframing is designed to include experience with the repudiated but specifically necessary alternative for problem-solving.

In his transferential relation with Freud, the Wolf Man identified projectively his own lack of worth in Freud. It was Freud who knew nothing about social reality. At the same time, the Wolf Man acted out and perpetuated his state of financial and social dependence and excessive sense of entitlement when he induced Freud to contribute materially to his economic well-being. Initially, this could be taken as an active and necessary action to supplement the Wolf Man in a critical failure. Since the behavior continued for some years and was identified as what had impeded the resolution of transference, it can be assumed that Freud had been induced to play the countertransferential role.

The Wolf Man consulted Freud, one of the most eminent therapists in Vienna at the time. He may have induced Freud to overvalue him. Surely, the analyst must have perceived him as a very special case in all senses of the word: socially, economically, and for the interest that he fostered in psychoanalysis. Initially, Freud was able to avoid the acting-out of the countertransference, but finally he was induced to the overprotective behavior that, according to Mack Brunswick, made him remit the case to her for further analysis. The Wolf Man implied how much Freud confused his transferential problem when he referred to the termination of his first treatment. Freud suggested that the Wolf Man buy him an expensive gift on termination of analysis because he thought that this would express the Wolf Man's gratitude and relieve his sense of guilt for having received so much (Obholzer 1982). One receives the impression that this request confirmed instead the Wolf Man's feeling that Freud, too, could be bought by his economic power. The Wolf Man was not the overgrateful type.

Two parental positions were available to the Wolf Man in his constricted problem space: (1) that of a mother—submissive, devalued, and dependent; (2) that of a father—dominating, devaluing, and dependency-creating.

The required therapeutic corrective experience was based on mutual interpersonal respect and consideration, on an encouraging financial and social autonomy, and on the development of skills to achieve this independence. The Wolf Man himself spoke to Obholzer about the dangers of the excessive dependence that he developed in transference with Freud. He criticized the aspects of psychoanalysis that reinforce dependence and "blind obedience" toward the therapist.

MUTATING THE REINFORCING ENVIRONMENT

A fourth source of resistance to overcome in the therapeutic process is that offered by a social environment that confirms the patient's behavior. When the subject tries to change, certain environmental pressures reward or punish him and maintain him within the socially shared understanding. This form of resistance is somewhat analogous to Freud's concept of secondary gain in that the subject receives some reward or confirmation for *not* changing, or for changing back to the acceptance of the social game and its rules; if he does not accept the social game, he is excluded and suffers punishment.

The importance of environmental consideration in therapeutic outcome is evident. The subject acts in a conceptual system that forms part of a family action system. This system, in turn, forms part of a larger social environment (Whiting 1963). The shared system is dyadic, consisting of two complementary positions in a game that itself is defined and valued in general terms by the society and the significant others. Therefore, the therapist should help the analysand question the game and find others who share the desire for and the values of a new game. The environment may have the power to impede change, even when the subject is lucid and aware of the social game. The analysand may be aware of it as a defensive game, but the new understanding in that situation is not relevant to the social reality and is not rewarded as if it contributed to shared happiness. The environment itself is defensive in its organization.

When the Wolf Man entered treatment with Freud, he brought his confirming group with him. He had a personal physician and a medical student with whom to play cards, as well as a valet to dress him. He was maintained financially, and the responsibility for his inheritance had been taken totally out of his hands until he reached the age of twenty-eight. He needed only to free associate and to recount dreams in order to be the favored son.

Freud destroyed this comfortable state when he placed an arbitrary time limit on treatment (1918). The Wolf Man was forced to take seriously his time with Freud in terms of a greater state of autonomy. If Freud had not modified the setting in order to change its meaning, the Wolf Man would have had no motivation to change. Analysis would probably have continued on indefinitely and the Wolf Man would have not been required to confront his anxieties.

FOUR SOURCES OF RESISTANCE IN THE THERAPEUTIC PROCESS

In summary, the strength of conviction is a key factor in resistance and in achieving change. Indeed, it is easier to develop a new understanding on an intellectual level than to hold this understanding with emotional conviction. To produce significant links, which are the source of conscious and unconscious motivation and to undo or compensate the existing historic unconscious motivational bond are major tasks of therapy.

We specify four sources of resistance to be addressed in the therapeutic process: (1) the *intraframe* resistance against making directly conscious what is known but inverted defensively in the constricted conscious space; (2) the resistance of the deep unconscious, where affect has been bonded to a certain type of interpersonal relationship that is reproduced compulsively in transference and in the melodramatic off-task behavior that consists of blaming or devaluing interpersonally while failing to address the underlying cause of his anxiety, a failure in some vital task; (3) the preconscious resistances as they relate to the *intraframe-extraframe* passage of the dissonant repudiated information; (4) an environmental resistance due to the shared nature of understanding, whereby the environment rewards the analysand when he acts the social game and obeys the social rules. These resistances are involved in the corresponding therapeutic tasks of: (1) reverting the direction of the melodramatic material; (2) making conscious the melodramatic incompetence; (3) opening the frame to the specifically absent but necessary inclusions; and (4) changing the pathogenic environment.

These four sources of resistance are major obstacles in the path to a healthy capacity to fulfill what is consciously desired. Therefore, the therapeutic procedures should take into account factors of power, potential unconscious representations absent but essential to free desire, and metaconscious lucidity to perceive and question the frame constrictions. They should also use the interpretations and explanations that permit a retaking of true identity; they should design and transmit the experience of the specifically therapeutic nontransferential relationship, both in therapy and in the larger environment: they should make an analysis of the pathological confirming environment and should prescribe and help to select or create a therapeutic environment that favors change.

14.

THE PSYCHIC SPACES
IN THERAPY

Here, we link the psychic spaces to the therapeutic tasks. We take the preconscious frame as the point that defines the important division between *intraframe* and *extraframe* tasks, as well as giving significance to the development of the *extraframe* metaconscious and potential unconscious spaces as they permit the use of paradigmatic psychoanalytic technique. The development of the metaconscious space is related inversely to the degree of dogmatization of the preconscious frame. The ability to recognize assumptions as such and to question them also depends on the development of the metaconscious. The potential unconscious space contains the representations specifically necessary for the analysand to reach a solution to his interpersonal and socioeconomic problems as well as the potential for the creative use of his increased freedom.

The following list summarizes the contrasts between the *intraframe* and *extraframe* tasks and technique.

Intraframe	*Extraframe*
Traditional psychoanalysis	Paradigmatic psychoanalysis
Working through	Working out
	Breaking through
	Enrichment
Present or excessively present in the analytic material	Absent from the analytic material but essential to solve real problems
Repression into the unconscious	Repudiation, active exclusion from the *intraframe* spaces
Signified in the *intraframe* conscious and unconscious	Represented in the potential unconscious

Return of the repressed	Return of the repudiated
Defense	Deficit
Pleasure principle	Reality principle
Change	Mutation
Reversing the roles	Changing the game
Minor resistance	Major resistance

The traditional task of pychoanalysis is to make conscious what has been repressed in the unconscious and to put ego where id had been. Repressed material tends to be present in the analysand's speech in a distorted form, but in the unconscious it is represented in a direct form. It is linked to affect, being signified in relation to the affect organizers of the unconscious. The repressed material returns from within and is manifest in the repetition compulsion or defensive melodrama. The melodrama obeys the pleasure principle and involves the unfair distribution of displeasure. The traditional psychoanalytic task of making conscious and working through this repressed material has to do with *intraframe* or *first order change*, a reorganization within the frame assumptions. In this process, roles are reversed and projections are introjected. The interpretations necessary for first order change, which deal with the superficial unconscious, meet with minor resistance.

In contrast, paradigmatic psychoanalysis does not stop with the task of making conscious the unconscious and working through this material. It includes the integration of what is essential to problem-solving and is not a part of the *intraframe* symbolic space. Such representations are notably absent from the analysand's speech and actions. When they are dissonant to the organizing assumptions of the preconscious frame, they are repudiated (actively excluded). Since this material is not repressed, it does not return from within; it returns from without. That is, it is essential to resolve an important external problem. The need for it appears in response to a situation outside the symbolic world. The need for its inclusion obeys the reality principle in that it is essential to deal competently with reality. When it is dissonant, and not simply absent in a neutral way, its introduction implies a second order change. The structure of interpersonal and social relations itself is to be changed. The inclusion of this repudiated material meets with strong resistance from the frame. The metaconscious space, from which the frame assumptions can be analyzed, allows accessablity to the *intraframe* space of these *extraframe* representations.

The task of paradigmatic psychoanalysis is much broader than that of traditional psychoanalysis. In its *extraframe* aspects, it revolves around an analysis of frame assumptions and the integration of these notably absent but essential signifiers. It also includes the development and use of the creative aspects of the potential unconscious. Working through the melodramatic defenses and working out the drama is followed by a breaking through to new possibilities. The inclusion of the repudiated allows a greater symbolic and pragmatic competence. There is no longer a failure on the level of the real and, therefore, no longer a return of the repudiated from without. Enrichment goes beyond the inclusion of the specifically absent. It is an opening to the creative potential that lies beyond the constrictions of the frame in the representations of the potential unconscious.

The following diagram (see Fig. 2) links the psychic spaces to the therapeutic material. We will organize our presentation of the techniques of therapy first in terms of the spaces and then in terms of logical sequence of the analytic tasks. Although this presentation involves a certain redundancy, it emphasizes the importance given to the psychic spaces in the theory and technology of treatment.

ANALYZING THE CONSTRICTED CONSCIOUS PROBLEM-SOLVING SPACE

Manifest material from the constricted conscious shows an excessive presence of the defensive melodrama. The identity of self and other are inverted, as is detectable by a comparison of the analysand's speech with his actions. Where the manifest conscious material is constricted in its content, specific and universal deficits are made apparent through the notable absence of certain material essential for the resolution of dilemmas and important problems. Reference to the dramatic problem that has created the traumatic level of anxiety is infrequently present, being mentioned incidentally or not at all in the manifest material. While it is infrequently present because attention has been defensively displaced to the melodrama, this material becomes manifest on direct questioning of the analysand or his significant other.

In times of the crisis that results from a vital failure and produces an overwhelming state of anxiety, there is an important accentuation in the constriction of conscious content almost exclusively to the sadomasochistic. The analysand talks repetitively about interpersonal mistreatment where

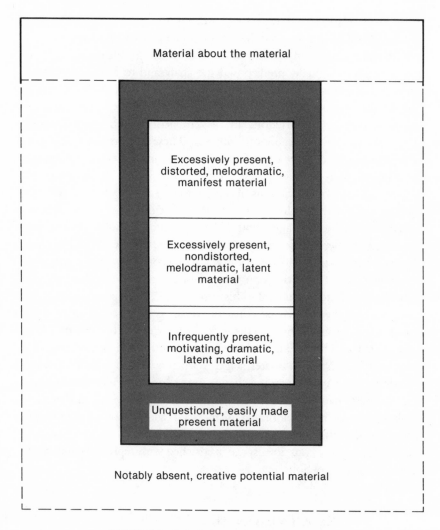

FIGURE 2. Dimensions of clinical material

he perceives himself as the victim or victimizer in his melodrama. This is why one always finds the melodrama to be excessively present early in the course of treatment. As the Wolf Man improved, he was able to dedicate himself to the relevant dramatic tasks of security, freedom, and happiness. When he was threatened into regression, he would talk almost exclusively about his own personal superiority. Improvement can be measured by the inclusion in the manifest material of references to nonsadomasochistic relations and to personal projects for creating happiness. That is, as the Wolf Man improved, he stopped talking about his superiority.

The constrictions on consciousness and on the problem-solving space are what have originally predisposed the analysand to a crisis of competence. A diagnosis of his problem-solving thinking and behavior form a part of the analysis of his constricted conscious space. The analysand suffers important constrictions in his convictions about self in both interpersonal and socioeconomic spheres. These constrictions may prevent him from seeing or using his own assets and potential, which is a prerequisite to his perceiving new goals.

The individual's convictions about himself as a person who can deal constructively with problems—that is, the conscious sense of self empowerment (Gear, Liendo, and Scott 1983; Bramucci 1980)—is extremely important in therapeutic outcomes. In the case of the Wolf Man, the negative, constricting self-concept in the socioeconomic area was that of a dependent role. The Wolf Man was unable to conceive of himself as a competing and successful rival to his sister.

In therapy, the constricted conscious space is analyzed in terms of its universal and specific deficits as these clearly interfere with initial problem-solving efforts. The defensive inversion of identity is first analyzed; displacement is resolved in a later stage. With the working through of the melodramatic defense, there is a change in the conscious manifest content. The manifest material distorted by inversion is reversed. The defensive displacement to the melodrama is replaced with a confrontation and working out of the dramatic problem. Finally, the frame constrictions are challenged, and the conscious space is enriched with representations from the potential unconscious.

RESOLVING THE SUPERFICIAL UNCONSCIOUS MECHANISMS

The representations of the superficial unconscious are evident in the latent material of analysis, which contains the direct representations of the subject's position in the sadomasochistic interpersonal game (dominating, defining sadist and submissive, defined masochist). The mechanisms of repression, projective identification, introjective identification, and denial produce an inversion of the direct coding of identity as the information passes from the *intraframe* unconscious to the *intraframe* conscious space.

As stated earlier, there is a resistance to truly changing the *dimensions* of the self-concept, even when the defensive inversion in conscious representation has been corrected. The forces against change do not stop with repression; there is a genuine external interpersonal dynamic relationship in which active selection, induction, and reinforcement are present in the interaction with the significant other. This situation tends to produce an external confirmation of the inverted perception of roles as well as of the game itself.

Melanie Klein (1975) distinguishes simple projection from projective identification. Pathology, unfortunately, does not limit itself to thought about and verbal expression of convictions. It involves actions that induce an inevitable confirmation of these convictions. For this reason, the therapist should accompany interpretations with therapeutic corrective actions. These can be in the form of environmental and therapeutic pressures that will reframe the conditions for analysis. The therapeutic setting controls the compulsive acting of the melodrama with others who are accomplices in the perpetuation of the analysand's pathology.

The therapeutic task in relation to the superficial unconscious is the working through of the melodrama in its aspect of inversion and its dilemma-producing constricting organization. The direct representation of identity of self and other is worked through, the dilemma that is related to the splitting into bipolar categories is resolved, and the defensive displacement to the melodramatic is corrected. The analysand is then in a condition to analyze the dramatic problem.

The therapeutic task of reclaiming the repressed and projected identity requires the analysis of speech and the comparison of speech with action. It requires that the analyst point out and give a historic interpretation of these observations. The timing of these interpretations will depend on the patient's capacity to handle anxiety and his emotional competence. Too much interpretation at the wrong time produces psychotic levels of anxiety or results in a somatic crisis. In addition, since they are not elaborated, the results of such overwhelming insights tend not to have a lasting effect on change. The defense of repression and projective identification return and the momentary massive insight is lost. When properly timed, resistance to making the superficial unconscious conscious tends to be relatively minor compared with that which occurs when dissonant *extraframe* information is introduced.

Betty resisted perceiving herself as a blaming and deceiving person. She had identified this projectively in her husband and analyst. As she showed increasing receptivity, this was pointed out and interpreted to her in terms of her historic relationship with her mother.

Obviously, the achievement of a task such as the working through of the melodrama is not limited to interventions on the level of the superficial unconscious. Working through requires frame analysis of the reduction of choices to two false possibilites and an analysis of the deep affect organizers in terms of the origins of the sadomasochistic motivation.

RELEASING DESIRE FROM DEEP UNCONSCIOUS COMPULSION

Deep unconscious representations can be detected in the latent content of clinical material through an analysis of dreams, free associations, and compulsive motivation. On the unconscious level, there are two types of compulsively motivating representations: motivation to avoid in relation to an overwheming anxiety provoked by a perception of incompetence; and a historic motivation for a certain type of interpersonal relation (sadomasochistic) that guaranteed survival to the masochist and guaranteed a reduction in displeasure for the sadist. In the face of overwhelming anxiety, the dependent child repeated a specific narrow, stereotyped, sadomasochistic response. In the face of a return of overwhelming anxiety, the adult compulsively repeats this particular response, the simplistic, historic, sadomasochistic solution to life-threatening anxiety. The solution is structured within a polarized space. Paradoxically, what the subject fears and attempts to avoid is precisely what occurs as an inevitable result of the action's being avoided. The more he attempts to avoid the feared incompetence, the more he perpetuates the crisis.

The Wolf Man's deep unconscious contained the representation of the catastrophic loss of his privileged position with his father as a result of the relationship with his competitive, aggressive, superior sister. The experience of this loss of a privileged position was accompanied by feelings of rage and panic. This content was repeatedly manifest in his dreams, his acting out, his transference, and his free associations. In simple terms, the Wolf Man had a compulsive motivation to avoid recognition of his inferior status. He had two perceived historic choices: to accept the role of valueless and inferior and suffer the intolerable anxiety or to prove somehow that his sister was the worthless and unlovable one. There was no game of security, respect for effort, and guaranteed lovability. He could only dedicate his efforts to consistently prove the other to be the inferior one. Paradoxically, this effort took his energy and attention away from games that would have increased a realistic sense of competence and self-worth—dramatic games capable of producing happiness. He was trapped in and by his defenses.

In the transactional sequence of his acted melodrama, the Wolf Man selected inferior partners and induced them to stay with him for his superior economic worth. This behavior avoided but at the same time perpetuated his underlying sense of personal inferiority. His anxiety continued since he proved himself only superior to "sluts" whom he could buy.

Historically, the Wolf Man's action was limited to two complementary sadomasochistic alternatives, neither of which was a solution: he could either have humiliated or have been humiliated. He had been forced to make a choice between two false alternatives. In such situations desire is freed from this paradoxical compulsion only by the subject's facing the fear of inferiority and working through the sadomasochism. Then the incompetence is worked out. The subject is thus freed from the historic motivation bonded to early experience.

Changing this deep unconscious motivation becomes the most protracted aspect of therapy. Change is resisted by melodramatic "acting out" behavior, which occurs whenever unconscious motivation exceeds the strength of the conscious motivation, especially in cases of threat to security. The real threat is simply not addressed. The subject will be found to defend strongly against the therapist's attempts to introduce discussions about the real failure, which he must confront in order to deal healthily with the source of anxiety. The analysand registers and attends the existence of anxiety, not the cause of the anxiety. He defends against this anxiety, rather than solving the problem that has caused the actual threat to his security. This defense increases the failure, closing the circle of the repetition compulsion. It could be said that he avoids paying the immediate price of health: that is, he avoids recognition and confrontation of his anxiety-producing failure, remaining in an indolent limbo. The cost is compounded by the avoiding behavior itself.

A highly important therapeutic problem related to the representations in the deep unconscious is the containment of this anxiety and the introduction of an awareness of the deficits that have predisposed to it. In this stage of working out, the problem is not simply one of introducing information; this must be offered in circumstances, in a form and at a time that allow it truly to enter the *intraframe* psychic spaces and to become a part of the system. That is, the defenses and resistances, not merely the deficits, are important considerations. When a patient is deeply threatened, he increases his defenses and resistances and his psyche becomes both rigid and impermeable. In addition, the affect-experience bond that produces motivation to the repetition compulsion cannot be undone simply by interpretation or by being expressed in words and made conscious. A therapeutic experience is necessary, in which the therapist assumes the role of the accompanying counterphobic, persuading and encouraging the subject to face the sources of anxiety and to *live* the disconfirmation of his fear. To do this, the therapist must have rapport, be able to design the specifically therapeutic experience, and help select or create the necessary disconfirming environment.

The Wolf Man entered treatment more to avoid anxiety than to confront it. He created an environment of accomplices to his illness, who included his personal physician, his valet, and a relationship with Freud, which he understood to be a simple matter of attending sessions to free associate, to talk about dreams, and to be protected from a need to confront his inadequacies. Freud had to force him to confront his reality, the pressure he exerted was to limit the duration of treatment. Setting is a very important therapeutic instrument, which Freud used very effectively in this case.

When a time limit was put on the relationship, the Wolf Man began the process of working out. He was faced with another dilemma: he could either confront the underlying causes of his illness in order to change his relationship to reality—with the help of the still-present Freud—or he could continue to avoid the confrontation, knowing that he would soon be alone, unable to deal with his reality and unprotected from it. Only under this type of pressure did he give up his defensive plan and begin to work on solving his dramatic problem. Betty initially failed to face her dramatic problem of a deep sense of failure as a valuable human being. She reenacted her melodramatic problem of hiding herself from discovery while seeking self worth in superficial sexual encounters. It was under pressure from her husband, after her defensive acting out was discovered, that she began to face her underlying problem.

In summary, the deep unconscious is related to the following important tasks in the therapeutic process: identifying and controlling the action sequence of the repetition compulsion; confronting the deep unconscious panic aroused by a vital incompetence; analyzing the incompetence and working it through. These tasks involve the analysis of deficits, defenses of displacement, and the overcoming of both affect and social resistances.

THE PRECONSCIOUS FRAME IN TREATMENT

The preconscious material is easily made present in the manifest content of the analytic material. Forming part of the implicit unexpressed assumptions which organize understanding, it tends to not be present spontaneously. Since it is taken as natural, as an assumption common to all, it is not commented upon. Making it consciously manifest is not resisted or defended against. The therapeutic difficulty is in overcoming the subject's resistance to changing these implicit assumptions. Since the paradigm is in fact socially shared, efforts to change meet with both frame and social resistances. For this reason, paradigmatic psychoanalysis analyzes the social resistances of the other and the environment, who are often perpetuating accomplices to mental illness. It reframes the analysand's frame, propitiating conditions for therapeutic alliances.

Analysis of the frame is associated with the task of breaking through frame constrictions and goes on to an opening for enrichment. The preconscious frame is a focal point in paradigmatic psychoanalysis because of its strategic functions. It organizes, as well as delimits, the *intraframe* conscious and unconscious spaces. It is a source of strong resistance to therapeutic alteration (second order change) because of dogmatic attitudes and because suppositions are taken as natural and socially reinforced. It is responsible for absences or exclusions from the problem-solving space. When the excluded material is affectively neutral, its inclusion meets with minor resistance. When the absent material is dissonant to the frame assumptions and repudiated by the dogmatic defense, the resistance to its inclusion is active and strong. On the syntactic level of the frame's organizing functions, it is responsible for universal deficits.

Overcoming social and frame resistances in order to correct specific and universal deficits and break through to the enrichment of the potential unconscious are steps beyond the limits of traditional analysis. They are, however, tasks included in the frame of paradigmatic psychoanalysis.

The preconscious is analyzed from the *extraframe* meta-analytic space, taking into account deficits and resistances. The frame is first opened to the *intraframe* inclusion of essential absent material and then to creative enrichment. Frame resistance to the inclusion of repudiated dissonant material is very great, whereas resistance to the affectively neutral is minimal.

Betty, for instance, strongly resisted signifying relations that were honest and supporting. Such relations were dissonant to her frame assumption that all humans belonged to a category of those who were either deceiving and dishonest or denounced dishonest deceit. She rationalized away the significance of supporting attitudes, perceiving them as clever dishonest attempts to take her in. She saw the new as if it were the same old thing. She showed resistence to the introduction of affectively neutral material such as absent social skills and the skills she would need to make her dream come true by becoming an assistant in a nursery school. An alliance with the husband was an important factor in the therapeutic setting. It gave strength to the therapeutic efforts to disconfirm the paradigm, and it consistently introduced the dissonant absent material on the level of action and experience.

THE METACONSCIOUS SPACE AND FRAME ANALYSIS

The metaconscious is responsible for the manifest existence of material about material. This material analyzes and questions the assumptions that give meaning to information. This metaconscious space is essential in both traditional and paradigmatic psychoanalysis. Recognizing the social nature of understanding, paradigmatic psychoanalysis requires the analysis of the context in which the coding and interaction take place; the socially shared nature of the assumptions must be considered. This type of *extraframe* analysis permits a more objective perception of frame assumptions as assumptions, not as irrefutable facts. In order to develop this space, however, the subject requires input from a lucid witness who does not totally share his assumptions. This witness may be a therapist or an observer who is an outsider in some way. The analyst is aware that, in analyzing the assumptions of the analysand, he does so from the perspective of his own assumptions. The analyst takes the perspective of an epistemologist. This implies a nonintrusive scientific attitude. The analyst is explicit about the existence of his own assumptions and does not impose them arbitrarily or clandestinely. It is the ideology of the analysand that is being clearly defined and studied.

The analytic metaconscious space is developed in the analysand in the course of analysis as he is exposed to an objective contrasting point of reference. The questioning of assumptions requires that the subject initially be made aware of his cultural and family game from outside the constrictions of the game.

The Wolf Man shared his assumptions with the society in which he was born. The game of superior privileged and inferior unprivileged was reinforced by his society, family, and confirming environment. His importance and personal worth were guaranteed by his social role as the son of an important and powerful aristocrat. In his family, his father acted on these assumptions and did not even prepare him to look after the family estate. In addition, the family servants gave him importance and privilege because of his inherited role.

Freud himself seems to have assumed the counter-transferential role of ceding privileges to the Wolf Man when he did such things as taking up an annual collection for him. Mack Brunswick, on the other hand, did not permit this type of action in her therapeutic relationship with him.

It is a clinical fact that a lucid challenge to assumptions generally meets with easy success in producing change in areas of low affect involvement —that is, at levels on which the coding is organized by logic. At these levels, the emotional signifance of the information does not threaten value-laden hypotheses and, therefore, is not dogmatized or rationalized. When the degree of conviction is not an impediment to change, the new information is integrated rapidly. In areas of strong affect involvement, however, the absent information is dissonant and could be said to be repudiated. It is actively excluded from integration into the frame. The resistance of the value and cognitive defense can be overcome only by an *extraframe* analysis from the metaconscious. This is essential for the overcoming of frame rigidity and impermeability and thus the increase of communication between consciousness and the potential unconscious.

The metaconscious is the lucid space. The existence of a lucid witness is important to its development. There were no lucid witnesses to the Wolf Man's growing-up years. The paradigm of understanding, in which he believed in his own privileged protection, was confirmed by his family

and social environment. In therapy, the development of the metaconscious is achieved by external questioning and by the suggestion of other
possible understandings. What is important is not simply the content of
the metaconscious at any given time; the important element is the meta-
attitude of questioning assumptions and defining context. Betty was unable to question her own assumption that the world was divided into self-
righteous blamers who punished and pursued and the deceitful, bad objects of this pursuit. She was not talked to. Her family was highly punitive. No one in the family dared to question the mother. The father was
not lucid. He was the mother's blind instrument of justice. In short,
Betty's metaspace was undeveloped.

To make the analysand conscious of his basic and limiting assumptions
requires an outside perspective that does not take these assumptions as
natural. Until he entered analysis with Freud, the Wolf Man was not
aware that he played a "superior-inferior" game with women who gave
him privilege and recognized his superiority because he bought them. He
was even less aware that there was another, better game to play. Freud
was the lucid, creative, and powerful witness, and he described and analyzed the Wolf Man's melodramatic game. That is, he served in therapy as
someone analogous to a "transitional object," creating a symbolic space
that had not been created in childhood. To the degree that he was able to
achieve this, the Wolf Man's narcissism could give way to an intersubjective understanding of relationships. In addition, he requalified Therese as
a valuable woman who loved him for himself. According to the Wolf
Man, Freud formed an alliance with him in regard to his marriage to
Therese, which allowed him to go against his mother's wishes. The more
general alliance that Freud sought was one in which assumptions were
challenged consistently from a more "objective" *extraframe* position of the
metaconscious.

The Wolf Man overcame the rigid persistence of his framing assumptions as a result of identifying and experiencing a new and therapeutic
relationship with Therese. Freud supported him in his requalification of
Therese and in his efforts to abandon the melodrama. Therese herself
encouraged him to face his fears and return to school. As a result of the
identification and analysis of the old game and the identification of the
potential for a new and therapeutic game, the Wolf Man's frame could be
expanded to include more productive behavior, more oriented toward
happiness. Indeed, he assumed responsibility for his Nanya and his mother

and seemed to have made important gains while Therese was alive. Her death, unfortunately, put him squarely back into his melodrama.

THERAPEUTIC ENRICHMENT FROM THE POTENTIAL UNCONSCIOUS

Potential unconscious representations are absent when treatment begins. Deducible from the analysand's thinking, they appear in the manifest analytic material in the course of treatment and consist of those representations specifically absent from—rather than latent in—the *intraframe* spaces but essential for the release of desire from the repetition compulsion and for the truly *extraframe* creative imagining.

Openness to inclusion of the *extraframe* representations is dependent on analysis of the frame. Upon overcoming the valuative and cognitive resistances, the subject can call more freely upon his potential unconscious—that intuitive, playful, analogic thought not constricted by the preconscious frame. In pathology, any alternative that is generated and is dissonant to the frame value structure is rapidly disqualified and rejected. Although it is made conscious, it is not integrated into the frame. The potential unconscious, like the metaconscious, may be relatively undeveloped in subjects who have confined their thinking to the known and who have condemned playfulness and nongoal-directed activity as bad, useless, or inferior—that is, who have dogmatically curtailed creative imagination. The imagining *function* is independent of the content that is imagined. Like the more objective perception of self, it forms a part of the *extraframe* spaces. These spaces are developed in the subject's learning experience with his significant others, although they are not a part of that which is organized and delimited by the preconscious frame.

The Wolf Man placed little value on the creative products of his potential unconscious. He seemed not to dare or desire to compete in many aspects of his life. He did not see himself as having important socioeconomic projects to develop. After Therese's death, he did not have significant love relationships. Later, his conscious project was to get rid of Luise; at the same time, his compulsive unconscious motivation was to continue in the relationship with her and to prove her to be inferior and exploiting. What he valued—if we define what is valued by what was motivating to him—was the melodramatic game with Luise.

The Wolf Man's experience must have included the successful completion of a socioeconomic or interpersonal project based on mutual respect
and worth and the production of the happiness that resulted from the
achievement of personal or group projects. Surely he had seen examples
of such projects, but they were not *signified*. By this we mean that they
were not linked to the organizing affects of his symbolic system; nor were
they part of the values of his preconscious frame. They had no emotional
meaning and were not motivating.

The potential for new desire, as opposed to compulsive motivation, is
developed in the potential unconscious. Here, fantasy can be played with
as an impulse is converted into a desire. (Free and playful imagining is a
socially learned and stimulated function, although it has biological limits.)
The potential unconscious is developed in relation to the other, who
assumes the function of an outside stimulus for play that can generate
possibilities and create symbols. This creative function is something like
the "reverie" of Bion (1965) or like Winnicott's (1971) "transitional
object." The significant other allows and encourages symbolic play, which
creates the potential space between self and the totally separate external
object (Kohut 1971). Thus, the creative function is developed as a process. The given content of the potential unconscious is less important
than the development of the potential unconscious process. The specific
symbols may be created, but first the process must be developed to create
them. A knowledge of these principles has influenced the development of
techniques for increasing personal creative capacity.

It is clinically evident that a person who cannot anticipate success or
use the imagination in relation to new objectives is unable to enrich his
potential for the achievement of happiness. He cannot develop commitment or a high degree of motivation and is unable to conceive potential
projects. In many cases, it is important to teach the client to exercise his
imagination in terms of desired outcome. What remains unimaginable
remains unachievable, and although it lies within the biological potential,
it will never be acted upon. The subject must dare to desire, overcoming
the resistance of the constricting frame and the constricted self-concept,
in both interpersonal and politicoeconomic areas.

In summary, the contents of the potential unconscious are excluded by
the frame defenses. The development of the imagining potential and the
analytic metaconscious space becomes another focus of the therapeutic
work. This is the possibility generating space that significantly determines
the possibility of therapeutic enrichment. The process and contents of the

extraframe space and how to articulate this space with the frame take the forefront in therapeutic considerations. Teaching a subject to imagine and to play with symbols is a part of the therapeutic process and technique.

The following diagram (see Fig. 3) describes graphically the relation of the therapeutic dimensions to the topical dimensions.

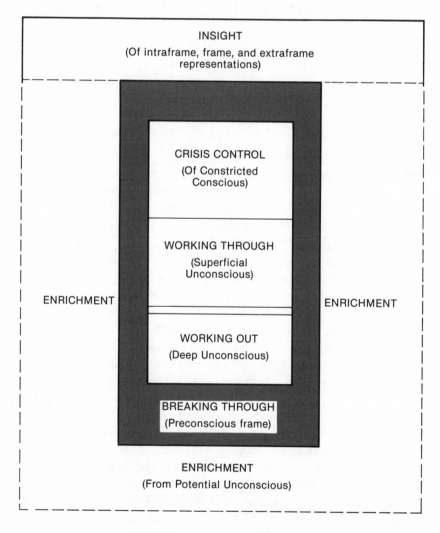

FIGURE 3. Therapeutic dimensions

15.

NEW DIMENSIONS IN
THERAPEUTIC TASKS

The therapeutic process itself can be divided into seven stages in which tasks are confronted sometimes sequentially and sometimes in parallel fashion. The analysis includes the factors that precipitated the crisis, those that predisposed to it and those that perpetuate it. In general terms, a crisis is precipitated by a mutation in the reality or in the personal condition of the analysand. This requires a corresponding change in performance that the analysand is unable to achieve. He, therefore, enters into a crisis of incompetence on a conceptual, emotional, or operational level. If his emotional reaction exceeds the level of a signal anxiety, he stops confronting the incompetence, escaping from the panic produced by the representation of his dramatic failure. His escape is to the lesser anxiety and displeasure of the representation of his defensive melodrama. The melodrama becomes a perpetuating factor in illness since it deviates attention from the resolution of the precipitating dramatic incompetence. The narrowness, closure, and schematic simplism of his frame, combined with his emotional incompetence, are the predisposing factors. Development is arrested since an evolutionary enrichment of the *intraframe* spaces cannot occur when the frame resistances are too great. Freedom and happiness are not produced when the psychic system enters into the defensive state. The analysand simply distributes unhappiness in an unfair sadomasochistic way. The therapeutic environment forming alliances in the projects for happiness, reinforces his healthy behavior. While the pathogenic environment reinforces the defensive behavior.

Therapeutic objectives coincide with the stages of treatment. The first stage is one of containing the crisis, reestablishing control of emotional incompetence. The second stage is a working through of the melodramatic perpetuating defense with the accompanying displacement of attention from the dramatic failure. The third stage is a working out of the predisposing deficits and a resolution of the drama. The fourth stage, which actually occurs in part in the working through and working out stages, is one of breaking through the frame constrictions. In this stage the frame resistances are analyzed from the metaconscious position. This is followed by a fifth stage of opening to and enrichment from the potential unconscious. The change the analysand may achieve is not stable unless there is a sixth stage environmental alteration. In this stage, the environment and significant others are in alliance for the production of happiness rather than in complicity in the unfair distribution of unhappiness. In the seventh and final stage, the analysand develops and puts into effect a new personal project for happiness to share with these others.

THE FIRST STAGE: CONTROL OF EMOTIONAL INCOMPETENCE

The usual immediate focus of treatment is the crisis of incompetence, precipitated by a significant change in the environment and/or the changed conditions in which the subject much reach his goal. The crisis of incompetence may be reflected chiefly in the internal or external aspects of functioning. When it is external, the crisis compromises the subject's interpersonal or politicoeconomic achievement. An internal crisis may be psychosomatic or psychological.

The first therapeutic tasks, therefore, are to deal with the traumatic anxiety and to help to rebalance the deficient functioning. The therapist also deals with the manifestation of failure, whether it be a somatization, a couple or family problem, or a socioeconomic crisis. The external change— the precipitating factor in the subject's reality—requires a corresponding updating of his actions and his paradigm of understanding. That is, the therapist deals with the cause and with the internal and external effects of the crisis, as well as providing emotional support to contain the subject's overwhelming anxiety.

The therapeutic process begins with the establishment of rapport. Rapport is easier to establish when the transference is positive. It depends on the therapist's capacity to feel and transmit empathy, acceptance and compassion, and it is aided by his capacity to anticipate and immediately to recognize the transference dynamic and to manage it in the patient's favor.

The analysand has suffered an emotional incompetence in which he is unable to maintain his anxiety at the signal level. He has entered into a state of traumatic anxiety in which he is defending himself against the anxiety rather than confronting the dramatic failure. To rebalance the system and contain the anxiety, the therapist resorts to an initial supplementing of the deficits that precipitate the melodrama. He also takes a complementary role in the analysand's sadomasochistic melodrama, assuming the role deliberately and in a measured way. In supplementing, the therapist or significant other uses his own capacity to compensate the failure on the level of the conceptual, emotional, and, to a lesser degree, operational deficits. The therapist calls upon the significant others in the environment to use their competence, especially emotional and operational, to rebalance the critically failing system. Complementing is done on the dynamic level. The therapist deliberately and consciously accepts the countertransferential role, allowing some acting of the melodrama in the initial stage. When the analysand's failure is compensated and anxiety is reduced to signal levels, then the dynamic therapeutic work can be undertaken directly.

The therapist analyzes the problem-solving functions of the analysand. He identifies specific and universal deficits and the problem to be solved, as well as diagnosing the general problem-solving behavior of the analysand. He does not involve the analysand in the meta-analysis of the problem-solving deficits at this point. He concentrates the subject on the problem itself, supplementing him when necessary in the detected deficits. At the later stage of working out, he will meta-analyze problem-solving with the analysand, involving him actively in efforts to correct the deficits.

On the conceptual level, the analyst notes the universal and specific deficits that impede problem solution. He notes the emotional strength of the analysand, his capacity to contain his own anxiety and to persist in problem-solving behavior in the face of difficulties and threatened failure. He notes the operational deficits that have contributed to failure. He does not yet give the subject insight into the deficit, but complements the deficit and later points it out to the analysand, helping him to find ways to correct or complement them.

It is difficult to evaluate accurately the patient's problem-solving potential until his melodramatic defense has been resolved. Some of our analy-

sands are unable initially to identify any problem and are referred to us
for somatic or social manifestations of an unidentified stressor. Such is the
case for alexithemics. They may experience vague anxiety, but they are
unable to connect it to any event. Others—the most numerous group—
come to consultation identifying a melodrama of blame or inferiority as
the problem. Their affects are appropriate to the melodrama, not to the
dramatic problem that precipitated their crisis. A third group comes to
consultation with the dramatic problem clearly identified and with the
affect appropriate to the drama that they are living. These people are
consulting because the magnitude of the event has created the need to
work through an important change or loss. They are emotionally competent, their anxiety is signal, and they are trying to solve their dramatic
problem. Such people can be evaluated in their problem-solving efforts
because they are dealing with the appropriate task, addressing the correctly identified problem. Those who are involved in their melodrama,
however, must first be directed toward the appropriate task and then be
further evaluated in their ongoing problem-solving functions. Those in
the first-mentioned group, who do not identify the problem and who
seem to have very little predisposition to introspection and to the study
of their own emotions, motivations, and perceptions, lack a developed
metaconscious process. In their case, the usual tools of analytic therapy
tend to be ineffective, because these tools depend on the existence of the
capacity to metasymbolize and on a developed potential unconscious
process.

The analysand is evaluated in his strengths, weaknesses and problems.
The initial evaluation allows a specific content to be given to the tasks
that are to be undertaken in therapy. It takes the following into account:

1. The dramatic change that precipitated the crisis of competence.
Does the subject identify the drama, or does he attribute the problem to
a melodrama? What are the new problems related to the change? What
skills are needed to solve the new problems? Is the affect that the subject
reports appropriate to the drama or is it the affect of a defensive melodrama? The Wolf Man, for example, consulted after he had been separated
from Therese because of her child's illness. Although he did not refer to it
as a cause for consultation, a major politicoeconomic revolution was
occurring in Russia. He did, however, ask Freud to advise him about
what he should do to defend his fortune, which he left in Russia. Freud
apparently also failed to identify clearly the factors that may have precipitated the need for consultation. According to the Wolf Man, he perceived

the relevant problem as that of resolving a transference remnant. Certainly the Wolf Man still transferred onto Freud the active, resolving role, while he remained in a dependent role and continued to idealize the power and wisdom of the father figure.

2. The cultural game. What melodramatic game is accepted and reinforced by the analysand's culture? What theme or cultural value does this game represent? How does the culture distribute displeasure unfairly? The Wolf Man's culture played the superior-privileged and inferior-underprivileged game, in which privilege was related to birth and not to social, economic, or political contribution.

3. The family and personal variation of this cultural game. How does the family interpret this melodramatic theme? The Wolf Man's family also played the game of superior-inferior, favored-humiliated. The father kept his son protected, but inferior and humiliated, while giving the superior and favored role to the competitive sister, who received his love.

4. Complementary roles. What are the complementary stereotyped roles played by the parents? What are the characteristics of the players and what is the relationship established between them? The two complementary positions—ego and alter—in this family melodrama. These have already been mentioned with respect to the Wolf Man: a superior, humiliating, abandoning, economically "protective" father and an inferior, humiliated, abandoned, dependent Wolf Man.

5. Assumed and assigned roles. Does he assume the interpersonal role of the dominating sadist or the submissive masochist? In the socioeconomic sphere, does he assume the role of the controlling agent or the dependent patient? To whom does he assign the complementary interpersonal and socioeconomic roles? The preferentially assumed role of the subject and the preferentially assigned role that he identifies projectively in the other, especially in relation to the interpersonal sadomasochistic role and the politicoeconomic role of control or dependence. The Wolf Man assumed the role of the dependent and helpless inferior other in his relation with his father and sister. He was comfortable, however, when he could perceive this role and identify it projectively in the other: in Therese, his Nanya and, at times, Freud.

6. Compulsive desire. What is the compulsive unconscious desire for avoidance that determines the interpersonal dilemma and the sequence of interaction, selections, and inductions of the repetition compulsion or melodrama. The Wolf Man was compelled to try to avoid the unpleasant recognition of his own inferior role, accompanied by the desperate rage and fear that this had provoked in him.

7. The acting of the melodrama. How was this achieved? In what sequence did the transaction occur? How did the analysand select the other and induce the countertransferential role? What was the feared outcome? The Wolf Man selected economically dependent people whom he could maintain and devalue, feeling that they would not abandon him because of their dependence. Then he treated them in a disrespectful way, proving that they could be bought and were inferior to himself and thus that he was superior. Even so, he could never resolve the desire to be loved and valued for himself, because the world was divided into the possibilities of submitting because of inferiority or of being submitted to because of superior economic power. The game did not include the possibility of being loved and respected for his human qualities, just for money.

The induction of the complementary behavior was fairly easy in Therese's case, but was impossible with Luise. She was too astute to be dominated by his gentlemanly manipulations; she managed to exploit and control him until his death. Therese, on the other hand, could help him break the paradox because she loved him and refused to be "bought" by his economic power; at the same time, she was not economically threatening to him. This situation changed his attitude and made him wish strongly to marry Therese. She allowed him the kind of experience that could help to reorganize his deep unconscious affects. Her death, unfortunately, exposed him again to an environment where the superior-inferior game was played in much more virulent terms.

8. The frame defense of dogmatization. What is idealized, and what is denigrated? To what degree is the frame impermeable to information? How is the lucid witness disqualified? What power does the lucid witness command? Do power alliances exist to support the lucid witness? What happens when the therapist tries to introduce dissonant, repudiated, but important information? The Wolf Man was taught to idealize the aristocratic role at the same time as he was taught to be dependent. He himself devalued Therese because she was uncultured and did not meet aristocratic standards. Freud experienced difficulty in persuading him that Therese was really an exceptionally valuable woman. The Wolf Man was quite dogmatic in accusing Freud of having given him bad advice and therefore of being responsible for his economic plight. He idealized authority and then held it absolutely responsible for any outcome. This attitude made it very difficult to introduce information about his own autonomy and personal responsibility.

9. The cognitive defense. What is taken as natural, and what is excused

with pseudological arguments? What is misperceived as if it were the same old thing when, in fact, it is new? The Wolf Man did not question the idea of his privileged birth until the time of his illness. He took as natural Freud's assumption of economic responsibilities toward him. He took as completely natural and unquestionable the idea that mental illness was related to insecurity and indecisiveness; he could not recognize that Therese, who was so decisive, had been severely depressed before her suicide.

10. The specific coding style and coding deficits. What are the coding strengths? What is deficient in the coding? Are digital functions low or high level? Are analogic functions low or high level? Regarding *extraframe* coding functions, are the meta- and potential unconscious spaces developed in terms of process? The Wolf Man was deficient in high-level digital functions; his style was strongly analogic. In terms of *extraframe* space, he was more able to analyze the assumptions of the other than to see his own. He did not have a great creative imagination, although he engaged in a great deal of stereotyped fantasy activity.

11. The affect resistances. What affect related to experience must the analysand achieve in a correctly identified, consistently lived therapeutic experience? Is this confirmed in the environment? The Wolf Man required a relationship of love and respect for himself, in which the partner would support his efforts to produce happiness to share with others. Therese came close to providing this relationship, but she suffered the disadvantage of dogmatic devaluation. She was considered inferior by the society, and she tended to devalue herself; thus to be loved and supported by her was not the same as being loved by an equal. The witnesses to the relationship, with the exception of Freud, devalued her.

12. Environmental resistances and facilitating forces. Who are the allies of the healthy aspects of the subject? Who are the members of the environment who are accomplices to the mentally unhealthy? How is the counter-acting out induced and rewarded by the environment? What type of environmental experience will be therapeutic? In his last years, the Wolf Man did have potential allies, who were lucid about his relationship with Luise. The strength of his unconscious compulsion, however, did not allow him to make the therapeutic alliance. With Therese, he had been more open to alliances with therapeutic elements.

13. Resources and assets. What resources are available? Are there economic resources? Is there motivational commitment? What interests and talents characterize the subject? What skills and resources are neces-

sary for the resolution of the actual problems? What resources are available for the fulfillment of new desire? The Wolf Man had economic resources and was able to return to the university. His father's will allowed him economic independence at the age of twenty-eight, the age at which he terminated his first analytic treatment with Freud and married Therese.

This dynamic evaluation, coupled with the listing of deficits, defenses, and resistances, gives the base on which the tasks of reversal of identity, challenge to the game itself, and the freeing of desire can be planned and undertaken.

THE SECOND STAGE:
WORKING THROUGH DEFENSES

The second stage is that of dynamic resolution of defenses. The defenses to be worked through are the mechanisms that result in the defensive melodrama and the accompanying displacement to the tolerable displeasure of sadomasochism. The melodrama depends on the use of seven unconscious intrapsychic mechanisms: repression, displacement, splitting, idealization, denigration, projective identification, and introjective identification. In the therapeutic process, repression is lifted and attention is given to the displaced. The third alternative, which is necessary to resolve the dilemma, is developed. What was identified projectively in the other is introjected. What was identified introjectively is projected.

The therapeutic operations for overcoming the melodrama begin by reversing the inverted perception of identity. By concretely showing, explaining, and interpreting transference, the patient is made conscious of the unconscious role that is apparent in his action. The analysis compares the description given by the analysand to his actions in the therapeutic situation and in the environment. This reclaiming of identity is unpleasant but not catastrophic in its emotional effect. The analysand has had experience taking the complementary role at times in his life.

To achieve the analysis, the melodramatic acting is reduced. The Wolf Man should have been controlled in his transference and paratransference relations where he attempted to confirm his superiority by contrasting himself with an inferior other who was economically dependent upon him. This controlling process often implies environmental interventions to create a therapeutic frame that operates on nonsadomasochistic as-

sumptions. The environmental complicity should be analyzed and resolved.

In addition, a meta-analysis of the historic family melodramatic game
is begun, in which the two complementary ego-alter roles are identified.
This identification is achieved by noting the subject's complementary
descriptions of self and others. This constricted conscious, polarized organization of roles and actions (splitting) is analyzed; it is linked to the
inverted ego-alter identity and to the dilemma the subject faces. We
believe this conceptual splitting and tendency to organize experience into
complementary classes to be responsible for the universal conceptual
deficit that underlies the dilemma with its forced false choices. Now the
dilemma is addressed on the logical level of thought and its consequent
action.

Specifically, the therapist labels the alternative position and action that
must be introduced from the representations of the potential unconscious.
That is, he demonstrates how the game can be ended and uses the
therapeutic situation to enact this nontransferential relationship. He has
both logically analyzed the transference and has introduced analogically
the experience of a specifically therapeutic nontransferential relationship.
The analysand no longer takes as natural the sadist's definition of who is
to be superior and entitled and who is expected to be inferior and unenti-
tled. Nor does he take the game itself as natural. He is aware of the
sequence of actions that always lead to the same outcome. That is, the
action resistance of the melodrama is overcome; the identity inversion is
rectified; the self-concept is enriched (Erikson 1956); and the universal
deficit of narrowness and of simplistic dilemma formation is addressed.

The Wolf Man's dilemma was that of choosing between being at least
accompanied because of his superior economic power or of being unloved
and abandoned because of the discovery of his inferiority. He could not
conceive of being loved and respected for his company rather than for his
money. When he found love and acceptance for himself in Therese, he
improved remarkably. His compulsive behavior was controlled, and he
returned to his studies. When he lost her, he suffered a severe regression
and returned to a denigrating sadomasochistic relationship with Luise.
With Therese he had not only resolved the splitting on a cognitive level;
he had lived the solution emotionally and pragmatically.

The analysand, like the Wolf Man, must experience a new affect related
to a new experience that balances, neutralizes, disconfirms, and gives an
alternative to the feared and anticipated outcome (the third alternative

that breaks the dilemma). This experience entails that, instead of playing the superior-inferior melodrama with him, someone conscious of his problem love and accompany him and, at the same time, encourage him in his efforts to produce happiness.

This new affect experience present in the therapeutic and paratherapeutic relationships should be identified, labeled, modeled, and presented consistently. The analysand should clearly identify the relationship and the emotion that both the relationship and his new attempts at producing freedom and happiness produce in him.

The historic power plays based on denigration and idealization are identified and analyzed. The sadist's definition of good and bad and his moral threat to the masochist if he does not play the game are identified. From this metaconscious position, the lucid witness analyzes with the patient the use of idealization and denigration to resist the inclusion of the repudiated dissonant material. The analysis includes demonstrating when, how, and why the sadist forces the masochist to stay within his role and within the limits of the game. The therapist must requalify the sadist's disqualifications.

The power of definition assumed by the sadist makes the therapeutic introduction of information more difficult than in the case of the masochist because the sadist does not readily assign the role of power to the therapist. Assuming the position of the definer is natural to the sadist. This is one of his sources of power. Therefore, a knowledge of power mechanisms (Lasswell 1930) and of the sources of therapeutic power is required in any analysis for a successful challange of the sadistic definition and for a rapid neutralization of the sadomasochistic escalations, excessively present in speech and action and so characteristic of the early stages of therapy. Betty was sadistic, dominating interpersonally. She felt the right to accuse and to judge. She behaved arbitrarily and aggressively. The therapist required an alliance with her husband to have the power to confront her on issues of sadism and to clearly challenge her on these assumptions.

THE THIRD STAGE: WORKING OUT DEFICITS

The subject is now ready to deal with the traumatic representation of his incompetence, which was defended against by displacement to the sadomasochistic representation of his melodrama and produced only minor anxiety. What the analysand most fears and tries to avoid is what happens to him repeatedly. The Wolf Man feared himself to be inferior to his sister. His fear made him avoid competition and failure to the degree that he became truly inferior in his development. In this stage of treatment, incompetence will be analyzed on three levels: emotional, conceptual and operational.

The emotional incompetence of the analysand has not allowed him to face his anxiety in terms of its source. The therapist accompanies him counter phobically, compensating his emotional incompetence to convert traumatic anxiety into a signal level. In this way, he can change the stereotyped self concept that perpetuates the drama. The subject should be accompanied as the Wolf Man was by Therese if he is to confront his anxiety about his own inferiority and manage to do something about it, as the Wolf Man when he dedicated himself to studies or painting. In this stage, it is important that the therapist encourage the analysand to go beyond emotional and conceptual analysis of the drama to its pragmatic solution. The dramatic problem is faced and the analysand takes action to resolve it.

On a conceptual level, the traumatic representation of incompetence has limited the self-concept, very often in the area of socioeconomic development. In this area, some patients do not conceive of themselves as in control of their own lives. Still others learn to limit themselves to a role of little compromise and commitment to realistically possible goals and thus consistently fall short of their potential for productivity and happiness. The socioeconomic incompetence is analyzed in its conceptual and operational aspects.

Other conceptual deficits that predispose the subject to failure include those related to coding style and problem-solving skills. The analysand's capacity to address problems is analyzed with him, and he is given "deficit sight," an awareness of these deficits so that he may correct or supplement them. The analysis of how he solves problems includes the following steps:

1. *Problem definition.* The analysand is observed in terms of his capacity to identify and formulate the problem. The initial formulation tends to be defensive.
2. *Gathering information.* The analysand should be evaluated in terms of his capacity to distinguish the relevant from the irrelevant, to act on essential information as opposed to waiting for

complete information. He should know where to find information and how to evaluate its validity. The therapist will note the presence or absence of these capacities and make the analysand conscious of them. They will either be compensated consciously or corrected through learning experiences.

3. *The listing and generation of options for solution.* Again, the analysand in his defensive phase is limited to the paradoxical, complementary options of his historic dilemma. When resistances are overcome and the dramatic problem is addressed, however, it will be found that the low-level digital thinker can list options but cannot generate them. The generation of new options depends on the use of the potential-unconscious symbolic capacity. This capacity, however, is not present in all analogic thinkers, but only in those who have a well-developed *extraframe* potential-unconscious process. When this function is absent or deficient, the therapist will develop it with the analysand just as he develops the meta-analytic space. Creative exercises may be helpful. Impulsive analysands, low-level analogic thinkers, do not take the time to explore possibilities; they stop thinking after they have generated the first option. Exercises for generating and listing options and for making logical decisions stimulate their thinking capacity and place time between the stimulus event and the reaction.

4. *Evaluation of options in terms of cost-gain desirability, risk, and feasibility.* Analysands may have a decision-making style that fails to evaluate the real outcome and acts on "wishful thinking." The analysand may take high risks. He may not evaluate at all, but may act on intuition or impulse. It is possible to teach decision-making processes and criteria and to practice them with those who are deficient in these functions.

5. *Decision-making.* Some analysands have difficulty deciding. They may be waiting for more complete information, although the relevant information is already in. In this case, they tend to be low-level digital thinkers. Others perceive decisions as absolute events, not to be reviewed or reevaluated. They are not sufficiently capable of trying things out and modifying decisions when it becomes necessary to do so. The therapist identifies the analysand's decision strategy. He makes clear the difference between adequate relevant information and complete information.

He points out that failing to decide is a decision that may be very costly. A tentative decision, when acted upon, brings feedback that allows an increasingly better base of information on which to make further decisions.

6. *Strategic and operational planning.* The analysand may not be able to see the totality and therefore may be unable to make good strategic plans. This is true for those who lack a capacity for contextual analysis. Others will fail on the level of planning the operational detail. Still others are accustomed to react rather than to plan and be proactive. These deficits are noted and are compensated consciously or corrected in therapy. The therapist will call attention to the total picture and the long-term effects of his decisions when this type of analysis is lacking in the analysand. He will call attention to the social context in which the analysand is deciding and acting. He will help the analysand to anticipate and prepare for events.

7. *Administration of operations and resources.* Some analysands have trouble administering resources; others, with developing alliances and obtaining resources; others, with the specific skills necessary to solve the problem. When such skill is lacking, the analyst will help the analysand to define where and why he is having this difficulty. He will help him to develop a strategy in which the analysand learns these absent skills or finds others who complement him and who provide strength in his area of weakness.

In summary, the problem-solving skills are reviewed for deficits. The therapist compensates these deficits actively in moments of crisis, but then the analysand is given "deficit sight" so that he himself can compensate or correct these difficulties.

Deficits on the operational level are also identified. The therapist encourages the analysand to learn and practice the skills that are necessary to the production of happiness.

THE FOURTH STAGE:
BREAKING THROUGH FRAME CONSTRICTIONS

The frame constricts the problem-solving space of the analysand in such a way that he is unable to include what lies beyond the preconscious organizing assumptions. The excluded representations lie in the potential unconscious. Inclusions may be classified into those essential for problem-solving and those that are nonessential but creatively enriching representations. The preconscious is a source of resistance to their entry. The resistance that should be broken through in treatment includes the mechanisms of dogmatization and rationalization and the tendency to take assumptions as unquestionable, natural, and the only possible belief to hold.

The Wolf Man saw his irrelevant defensive melodrama as natural and did not question his narrow assumptions. If his understanding was questioned, the denouncing lucid witness was himself in danger of being devalued and considered too "inferior" to be taken seriously. When Obholzer (1982) requalified the Wolf Man's writing as valuable, he disqualified her statement as "vain." He perceived her as not capturing how things really were.

In treatment, the unquestioned pathological perception is challenged. The analysand has taken as natural what is pathologically limiting, and he does not see other things because his cognitive set makes him misinterpret them. He does not recognize that they represent a totally new class of experiences. The therapist attempts to consistently challenge these misperceptions and to make the analysand aware that he might look for something beyond what he routinely expects to find.

He also challenges dogmatic disqualifications. To do this requires power as well as lucidity. An important therapeutic task is to develop the power and credibility to requalify the analysand's productive efforts and to effectively disqualify his dogmatic disqualifications, as in the case of the Wolf Man. The therapist's power comes from his status, his skills, his alliances, and his role as an expert or an authority. His power makes him able to impose a therapeutic frame.

With Betty, the therapist had to use his reputation as a serious professional, his skill in handling the countertransference, and his alliance with the husband in order to have the power to challange Betty's assumptions. This was done within a clearly designed therapeutic frame which did not consider Betty as the only variable. Her significant others were included in the therapeutic plan. Betty took deceit as natural and dogmatically resisted the inclusion of repudiated information about sincere relationships. Given her resistance, the therapist required clarity, power, and persistence in the efforts to reframe and to help her to overcome her dogmatic attitude. It also required the collaboration of her husband.

Rationalization allows the analysand to explain away the information he perceives as dissonant to his assumptions. Other dissonant experiences may be registered as different but are considered the exception that does not change the rule. Their significance is not registered.

To break through frame resistances requires power and lucidity. Power is required to requalify the disqualified. An *extraframe* metaconscious perception is essential for the analysand to appreciate that assumptions must be questioned. Analysands become more aware of their assumptions as their metaconscious space is developed in the course of analysis. Challenged on the level of logic, the rationalizations of the analysand are transformed into reasoning.

All representations in the potential unconscious do not meet with the same degree of resistance. Those that are affectively neutral enter without resistance. Those that are dissonant to the frame assumptions are strongly resisted. Their integration implies a reorganization of the valuative as well as the cognitive system. Their recognition implies experiencing the emotional chaos and anxiety of the subject's recognizing that he doesn't understand. The analysand realizes that he is unable to anticipate and does not have an action plan that will be effective in dealing with what comes. Repudiated material meets with the greatest resistance. It is actively selected out. In treatment much of what was actively selected out must be equally actively selected in.

THE FIFTH STAGE:
OPENING TO UNCONSCIOUS ENRICHMENT

When the frame defenses are overcome and desire is freed from the repetition compulsion, the analysand is open to reevaluate and explore his own potential. What are his assets, abilities, values, needs? Now he can look outside and forward into the future, not merely inside and backward into the past.

The analysand explores possibilities, using the less constricted imagining and the information available in his potential unconscious and in his new relations with the environment. This is a moment of "wishcraft." Truly free playful associations are encouraged. The therapist tries to induce the analysand to suspend his evaluating judgments and to help him to generate options. By favoring and teaching free associations, he helps the analysand retake his capacity for creative enriching thought.

NEW DIMENSIONS IN THERAPEUTIC TASKS

Fantasy and imagining of the desired future are undertaken; the analysand takes time to think about what makes him happy.

THE SIXTH STAGE: ENVIRONMENTAL CHANGE

The environment and the significant other are usually accomplices in the perpetuation of illness. The melodrama is played out in a complementary dyadic relationship with another who confirms the suppositions of the analysand. When the analysand tries to change the relationship to a more healthy one, he may find that the significant other pressures strongly for him to return to his former behavior. The significant others must often be included directly in treatment to attenuate their tendency to melodramatic complicity. At times the analysand is able to analyze the relationship, his own inductions, and reinforcements and to modify them indirectly without the direct participation of the significant other. To modify the environment requires power as well as lucidity. The analysand learns to select others who are allies to him in his healthy actions. He may have to distance himself from those who cannot change and who are pathogenic.

In relation to the larger environment, the analysand may create a micro-environment of others who share his productive concerns. He certainly will take the environment into account and will modify it, or select a more healthy one, to the degree that this is possible. This, at times, implies changing a work environment or community affiliations.

Environmental analysis and transformation form an important part of paradigmatic psychoanalysis. These may be accomplished through direct contact with significant others or indirectly through the analysand.

THE SEVENTH STAGE: THE NEW PROJECT

Having developed a new desire and an environment commensurate with the achievement of this desire, the analysand must now plan strategically and operationally and act upon the plan. Here his problem-solving skills are important. These are analyzed specifically, and his deficits in thinking style are taken into account.

The newly imagined and newly desirable is now reality—tested in terms of feasibility, probability, cost and gain. The analysand evaluates what he has explored; he reality-tests his options in relation to his desires. The objective is to develop a concretely and specifically new personal project that takes into account the personal desire and the external opportunities.

The analysand himself makes specific and concrete plans on both the strategic and operational levels for the fulfillment of what is newly desired. The organizational and problem-solving skills that are diagnosed as deficient, in both the analogic and the digital modes, must be developed or supplemented. This step is essential to the real fulfillment of desire. Finally, results must be evaluated and action plans revised in accordance with the result.

Having worked with the analysand on his plan and having established the personal project, the therapist encourages the analysand, gives him feedback, warns him about getting off the track, and encourages him to try to evaluate his behavior himself. With this step the analysand has prepared himself to fulfill his healthy, realistic desire. Treatment has included both the resolution of *intraframe* medodramatic problems, the working out of the dramatic problem, the breaking through of frame constrictions, and the development of the *extraframe* potential for resolving dramatic problems and freeing and fulfilling desire.

REFERENCES

Abramson, N. 1966. *Information theory and coding*. New York: McGraw-Hill.

Adams, J. S. 1965. Inequity in social exchange. In *Advances in experimental psychology,* ed. L. Berkowitz. New York: Academic Press.

Adler, A. 1955. *Le tempérament nerveux*. Paris: Payot.

Argyris, C., and D. Schon. 1974. *Theory in practice: Increasing professional effectiveness*. San Francisco: Jossey-Bass.

Asch, S. E. 1955. The doctrine of suggestion, prestige and invitation to social psychology. *Psychological Review* 250–76.

———. 1952. *Social psychology*. Englewood Cliffs, N.J.: Prentice-Hall.

Aylesworth, T. G., and G. M. Reagan. 1966. *Teaching for thinking*. Garden City, N.Y.: Doubleday.

Backman, C. W., P. F. Secord, and J. Pierce. 1963. Resistance to change in the self concept as a function of perceived consensus among significant others. *Sociometry* 26:102–11.

Barthes, R. 1967. *Elements of semiology*. London: Jonathan Cape.

Berliner, H. J. 1977. Some necessary conditions for a master chess program. In *Thinking: Readings in cognitive science,* ed. P. N. Johnson-Laird and P. C. Wason. Cambridge: Cambridge University Press.

Bieri, J., and S. Masserley. 1957. Differences in perceptual and cognitive behavior as a function of experiential types. *Journal of Consulting Psychology* 21: 217–21.

Bion, W. R. 1965. *Transformations*. New York: Basic Books.

———. 1967. *Second thoughts*. London: Heinemann Medical Press.

Bloom, Allan. 1987. *The closing of the American mind*. New York: Simon and Schuster.

Bogen, J. E. 1975. Some educational aspects of hemispheric specialization. *U.C.L.A. Education* 17: 24–32.

————. 1962. Cerebral commisurotomy in man: Preliminary case report. *Bull. Los Ang. Neuro. Soc.* 27: 169–72.

Bramucci, R. 1980. Self empowerment. Ph.D. diss., University of Oregon.

Brehm, J. W., and A. R. Cohen. 1966. *Explorations in cognitive dissonance*. New York: Wiley.

Brim, O., and W. Stanton. 1966. *Socialization after childhood*. New York: Wiley.

Bruner, J. S. 1947. International research on world issues: A world survey. *Journal of Social Issues* 3: 38–53.

————. 1973. *Beyond the information given*. New York: W. W. Norton.

Cicourel, A. 1973. *Cognitive sociology*. London: Macmillan.

Clausen, J. A., ed. 1968. *Socilization and society*. Boston: Little, Brown.

Cook, K. 1975. Expectations, evaluation, and equity. *American Sociological Review* 40: 372–88.

Cook, K., and R. M. Emerson. 1978. Poverty, equity, and commitment in exchange relations. *American Sociological Review* 43: 721–39.

Cooper, A. M. 1983. New issues in psychoanalysis. In *Psychiatry update*, ed. L. Grinspoon. Washington D.C.: American Psychiatric Press.

Deutsch, M. 1975. Equity, equality, and need: What determines which value will be used as the basis of distributive justice. *Journal of Social Issues* 31: 137–49.

Deutsch, M., R. M. Krass, and N. Rosneau. 1962. Dissonance or defensiveness? *Journal of Personality* 30: 16–28.

Diekman, A. 1971. Bimodal consciousness. *Archives of General Psychiatry* 25: 481–89.

Edwards, B. 1979. *Drawing on the right side of the brain*. Los Angeles: J. P. Tarcher.

Emerson, R. M. 1962. Power-dependence relations. *American Sociological Review* 27: 31–41.

Erikson, E. H. 1956. The problem of ego identity. *American Psychoanalytic Association Journal* 4: 56–72.

Festinger, L. 1975. *A theory of cognitive dissonance*. Evanston, Ill.: Peterson Row.

Feuerstein, R., and Y. Rand. 1974. Mediated learning experiences: An outline of the proximal etiology for differential development of cognitive functions. *International Understanding* 9 (10): 7–37.

Freud, S. 1895. The project for a scientific psychology. In *Standard edition of the complete psychological works of Sigmund Freud,* vol. 1. London: Hogarth Press.

———. 1900. The interpretation of dreams. *Standard edition,* vol. 4–5.

———. 1912. The dynamics of transference. *Standard edition,* vol. 12.

———. 1914. Remembering, repeating, and working through. *Standard edition,* vol. 12.

———. 1915a. Papers on metapsychology. *Standard edition,* vol. 15.

———. 1915b. The unconscious. *Standard edition,* vol. 14.

———. 1918. From the history of an infantile neurosis. *Standard edition,* vol. 17.

———. 1920. Beyond the pleasure principle. *Standard edition,* vol. 17.

———. 1923. The ego and the id. *Standard edition,* vol. 19.

Gardiner, M., ed. 1971. *The Wolf Man: With the case of the Wolf Man by Sigmund Freud.* New York: Basic Books.

Gear, M. C., L. Grinberg, and E. C. Liendo. 1976. Group dynamics according to a semiotic model based on projective and counterprojective identification. *Group Therapy.*

Gear, M. C., M. Hill, and E. C. Liendo. 1981. *Working through narcissism.* New York: Jason Aronson.

Gear, M. C., and E. C. Liendo. 1975. *Sémiologie psychanalytique.* Paris: Minuit.

———. 1976. Psychanalyse de la communication familiale. *L'évolution psychiatrique* 2: 240–72.

———. 1979. *Action psychanalytique.* Paris: Minuit.

———. 1980. *Psicoterapia della coppia e del gruppo familiare.* Florence: Del Riccio.

———. 1981a. *La thérapie familiale psychanalytique.* Paris: Dunod.

———. 1981b. Metapsychology of sadism and masochism. A bipolar semiotic model. *Psychoanalysis and Contemporary Thought* 4: 207–50.

———. 1982. *El lenguage y el inconsciente freudiano.* Madrid: Siglo XXI.

Gear, M. C., E. C., Liendo, and L. L. Scott. 1983. *Patients and agents.* New York: Jason Aronson

———. *Dream fulfillment.* 1988. New York: Jason Aronson.

Gergen, K. J., M. Greenberg, and R. Willis, eds. 1980. *Social exchange: Advances in theory and research.* New York: Plenum Press.

Glauser, D. 1978. *La naturalization symbolique*. Ph.D. diss., Université de Genève.

Glasser, R. 1971. *The nature of reinforcement*. New York: Academic Press.

Guilford, J. P. 1967. *The nature of human intelligence*. New York: Mc-Graw-Hill.

Harrison, A. F., and R. M. Bronson. 1983. *Styles of thinking: Strategies for asking questions and solving problems*. Garden City, N.Y.: Anchor Press.

Hartmann, H. 1964. *Essays on ego psychology*. New York: International Universities Press.

Horowitz, M. J. 1977. *Image formation and cognition*. Englewood Cliffs, N.J.: Prentice-Hall.

Jones, E. 1955. *The life and work of Sigmund Freud*. New York: Basic Books.

Jung, C. G. Ed. 1964. *Man and his symbols*. New York: Doubleday.

———. 1977. *The collected works of C. G. Jung*, vol. 6, series 20. Princeton: Princeton University Press.

Kagen, J., and N. Kogan, 1970. Individual variation in cognitive processes. In *Carmichael's manual of child psychology*, vol. 1, ed. P. H. Musser. New York: Willey.

Klein, M. 1975. *Writings of Melanie Klein*. London: Hogarth Press.

Kohut, H. 1971. *The analysis of the self.* New York: International Universities Press.

Kolb, D. A. 1984. *Experiential learning: Experience as the source of learning and development*. Englewood Cliffs, N.J.: Prentice-Hall.

Kolberg, L. 1963. The development of children's orientations toward moral order. *Vita Humana* 6: 11–33.

Kuhn, T. S. 1970. *The structure of scientific revolution*. Chicago: University of Chicago Press.

Lacan, J. 1966. *Ecrits*. Paris: Editions du Sevil.

Lakatos, I., and A. Musgrove. 1968. *The problem of inductive logic*. Amsterdam: North Holland Press.

Laplanche, J., and S. Leclaire. 1961. L'inconscient: Une étude psychanalytique. In *L'inconscient,* ed. H. Ey. Paris: Desclee de Brower.

Laplanche, J., and J. B. Pontalis. 1968. *Vocabulaire de la psychanalyse*. Paris: Presses Universitaires de France.

Lasswell, H. D. 1930. *Psychopathology and politics*. Chicago: University of Chicago Press.

Lerner, M. J. 1975. The justice motive of social behavior: Introduction. *Journal of Social Issues* 31: 1–19.

Lewin, K. 1951. *Field theory in social science.* New York: Harper and Brothers.

Luchins, A. S., and E. H. Luchins. 1950. New experimental attempts at preventing mechanization in problem solving. *Journal of General Psychology* 42: 279–97.

Marx, M. 1963. The general nature of social construction. In *Theories of contemporary psychology.* New York: McGraw-Hill.

McCarthy, B. 1980. *Teaching to learning styles with right/left mode techniques.* Barrington, Ill.: Exel Inc.

Messick, S. 1976. *Individuality in learning.* San Francisco: Jossey-Bass.

Nebes, R. D. 1974. Hemispheric specialization in commisurotomized man. *Psychological Bulletin* 81: 1–14.

Neri, C. 1982. Le microallucinazioni. *Gruppo e Funzione Analitica* 2: 21–34.

Newell, A., and H. A. Simon. 1972. *Human problem solving.* Englewood Cliffs, N.J.: Prentice-Hall.

Obholzer, K. 1982. *The Wolf-Man sixty years later: Conversations with Freud's controversial patient.* New York: Continuum.

Ogden, T. H. 1985. On potential space. *International Journal of Psychoanalysis* 66: 129–40.

Piaget, J. 1970a. *Genetic epistemology.* New York: Columbia University Press.

———. 1970b. *Structuralism.* New York: Basic Books.

Popper, Karl. 1972. *Objective knowledge: An evolutionary approach.* Oxford: Oxford University Press.

Rank, O. 1928. *Le traumatisme de la naissance.* Paris: Payot.

Rokeach, M. 1960. *The open and closed mind.* New York: Basic Books.

Rudner, R. S. 1966. *Philosophy of social science.* Englewood Cliffs, N.J.: Prentice-Hall.

Sartori, G. 1969. Politics, ideology, and belief systems. *American Political Review* 63: 2–21.

Seligman, M. E. 1975. *On depression, death, and development.* San Francisco: Freeman.

Singler, J. L., H. Wilensky, and V. Craven. 1956. Delay capacity, fantasy, and planning ability: A factorial study of some basic ego abilities. *Journal of Consulting Psychology* 20: 375–83.

Slawski, C. 1974. Evaluating theories comparatively. *Zeitschrift für Sociologie*. 3: 397–408.

Sperry, R. W., M. S. Gazzaniga, and J. E. Bogen. 1969. Interhemispheric relationships: The neocortical commissures, syndromes of hemispheric disconnection. In *Handbook of clinical neurology*, ed. P. J. Vinker and G. W. Bruyn. Amsterdam: North Holland Publishing.

Ten Houton, W. D., K. D Hoppe, J. E. Bogen, and D. O. Walter. 1985. Alexithymia and the split brain. *Psychotherapy and Psychosomatics* 43: 202–8.

Torrence, E. P. 1984. *Your style of learning and thinking*. Athens: University of Georgia Press.

Viderman, S. 1970. *La construction de l'espace analytique*. Paris: Denoel.

Walker, E., and R. W. Heyns. 1967. *An anatomy for conformity*. Belmont, Mass.: Brooks Cole.

Wason, P. C. 1968. On the failure to eliminate hypotheses: A second look. In *Thinking and reasoning*, ed. P. C. Wason and P. N. Johnson Laird. Hammondsworth, England: Penguin.

Watzlawick, P. 1978. *The language of change*. New York: Basic Books.

Watzlawick, P., J. H. Weakland, and R. Fisch. 1974. *Change*. New York: W. W. Norton.

Weiss, R. F., W. Buchanan, L. Alstatt, and J. P. Lombardo. 1971. Altruism is rewarding. *Science* 171: 1262–63.

Whitehead, A. N., and B. Russell. 1910. *Principia mathematica*, 2d ed. Cambridge: Cambridge University Press.

Whiting, B. B., ed. 1963. *Six cultures: Studies of child learning*. New York: Wiley.

Winnicott, D. W. 1971. *Playing and reality*. London: Tavistock.

Zajonc, R. B. 1980. Feeling and thinking: Preference needs no inference. *American Psychologist* 35 (February): 157–75.

INDEX

Abramson, N., 38

Abreaction, 126

Absent representations, 5–6, 60, 78, 79; and preconscious frame, 38, 39, 43; and therapeutic task, 134, 135; and work with the potential unconscious, 17, 21, 24, 26, 27, 33

Action mode, 121, 125, 126, 139

Adams, J. S., 60, 77

Adler, A., 80

Affect, 4–5, 6, 26; and analogic code, 85, 86, 93, 96–97, 98–100, 105–10; and deep unconscious compulsive desire, 62; and dual coding, 104, 105–10; and repressed material, 135; and resistance, 126–33; and therapeutic task, 158–59

Affect resistances, 6, 7, 156

Alexithymia, 93, 104

Analogic primary process, 4, 66–67; and affect, 85, 86, 93, 96–97, 98–100, 105–10; coding function of, 85–89; and compulsive desire, 105–10; conceptual and perceptual components of, 92–93; and creativity, 33, 86, 89, 94, 97; and health, 89, 97; therapeutic implications of, 73, 109–10. *See also* Dual coding

Analytic space, 69, 72

Anxiety, 6, 31, 34, 70; and growth process, 108; melodrama as defensive response to, 3–4, 30, 108; and precon-

scious functions, 35, 36, 38, 39, 46; and problem-solving, 55; and representations in the deep unconscious, 140, 141–43; and resistance, 128–29; and therapeutic process, 113, 114, 116, 118, 128–29, 139, 140, 141–43, 152, 153, 160

Argyris, C., 114

Asch, S. E., 80, 121

Assumed and assigned roles, 79, 154

Aylesworth, T. G., 86

Backman, C. W., 77

Barthes, R., 20

Berliner, H. J., 91

Bion, W. R., 70, 97, 98

Bipolar opposites, 24, 32; and preconscious frame, 43–44; and problem-solving, 49–52; and roles in melodramatic games, 79; and stereotyped contents of the unconscious, 60; and therapeutic process, 115–16

Blame and devaluation themes, 3, 6, 24, 50–51, 119, 129. *See also* Denigration

Bloom, Allan, 38

Bogen, J. E., 4, 48, 93, 104

Brain hemispheres. *See* Dual coding

Bramucci, R., 138

Brehm, J. W., 74

Brim, O., 37

Bronson, R. M., 86, 101

Bruner, J. S., 20, 35, 37, 100, 107, 126

173